The American Future

(What Would George and Tom Do Now?)

The American Future

(What Would George and Tom Do Now?)

by
William Van Dusen Wishard

Published by
The Congressional Institute, Inc.

316 Pennsylvania Ave. S.E. #403
Washington, D.C. 20003

FIRST EDITION

Library of Congress Cataloging-in-Publication Data

Wishard, William Van Dusen, 1930-

The American future: What would George and Tom do now? / by William Van Dusen Wishard

p. cm.

Includes bibliographical references.
ISBN 0-9633057-0-0
1. United States—Economic conditions, 1945- 2. United States—Economic policy. 3. United States—Social conditions, 1945- 4. United States—Social policy. 5. National characteristics—American. 6. United States—History. I. Title.

HC106.5.W574 1992
330.973'092—dc20 92-11061
CIP

To my father,
Charles Scoville Wishard,
whose love and thoughts along the way
are the seedbed of any truth this book
might contain. Ours was one of the
pioneer families that built America.

***

*"Americans are still inventing what it is
to be an American"*

— Thornton Wilder

CONTENTS

ACKNOWLEDGEMENTS

It is impossible to express adequately the debt I owe to those who, in one way or another, have been part of this book's creation.

To Jerry Climer, President of the Congressional Institute, whose experience in Congress is exceeded only by his vision of a Congress for the 21st Century.

To Bob Okun, Assistant Secretary of Education for Legislation and Congressional Affairs, who sees the possibility of a new governance for America.

To Frank Gregorsky, whose friendship and questing mind have seen, understood and encouraged when others still did not know what the questions were, and whose sharp eye skillfully edited this book.

To Jim and Ellie Newton, John and Denise Wood, and Tap and Frances Steven, whose ageless spirits see the promise of a new America in the making.

Most of all, to my wife Anne, whose courage and faith have made our journey into the unknown possible. Her spirit is written into every page of this book.

To all of these, I am grateful beyond my powers of expression.

PREFACE

SEARCHING FOR THE AMERICAN GRAIL

As America and Americans begin our journey to the 21st Century, an array of authors try to map out the road ahead.

In a comprehensive intellectual argument, **Allan Bloom** introduced the nation to the idea that some critical faults had crept into our way of thinking; he painted a picture of an intellectually bankrupt educational system in *The Closing of the American Mind* (Simon & Schuster, 1987).

Peter Drucker defined the new challenge facing business at home and abroad in *The New Realities* (Harper & Row, 1988).

Alvin and Heidi Toffler expanded upon the global nature of change in *Powershift* (Bantam Books, 1990); they challenged readers to admit that life beyond the post-industrial "third wave" was going to be different, whether we liked it or not.

Other writers — from **Gordon Jones** and **John A. Marini** in *The Imperial Congress: Crisis in the Separation of Powers,* to **E.J. Dionne Jr**. in *Why Americans Hate Politics,* to **P.J. O'Rourke** in *Parliament of Whores* — have painted pictures of broken institutions that force us to laugh, even if only to avoid crying or cursing.

Chaos in our thoughts, our institutions, our confidence has even led us, despite its explicit business focus, to **Tom Peters'** *Thriving On Chaos.* (The fact that the relentlessly can-do Peters defines every problem as an opportunity, and conveys both in blunt prose, helps us to stay tuned.)

Some have attempted to give us the answers to dilemmas we face individually and collectively. Others have been satisfied to outline our conditions. A few tried to make us laugh.

And then comes **William Van Dusen Wishard,** at just the moment we need him most. Wishard, in the work you hold in your hands, does not focus on answers. Though he defines certain social problems in new and stark ways, he will not add much to your horror-story arsenal.

Instead, "Van" Wishard offers a balanced, wide-angle view of who we are, how we got to be this way, and what we must do to solve our own puzzle. His perspective on the 1950s may fly in the face of conventional wisdom as it radically interprets that decade. But, as is often the case, what is served up here may do us more good than a restatement of conventional wisdom.

What Wishard really does in this book is to send us on our own personal journey by asking the right questions. Even there, to avoid lecturing or closing off new avenues, he does not call them questions; instead, he offers nine assumptions about Americans and the United States — and then encourages each reader to see if those assumptions are suitable for a 21st-Century Earth, as well as for that reader's own special American Dream.

Like all quests for the Holy Grail, the death of one adversary does not a victory make. The recent demise of the "evil empire" has not rendered universal happiness, wealth and prosperity for Americans — and it certainly won't for other citizens of the world.

In fact, rather than simplifying life, the dissolution of the Soviet Union may have complicated matters: We Americans have lost the clearest and most long-running good-guy/bad-guy contrast we ever had.

But *American Future* is no tale of U.S. international relations. It's much broader, just as the conditions affecting our lives are much broader. In fact, that is the secret to look for as you read. This book is about what is in us, not about what affects us.

Wishard heeds America's roots: His outstandingly concise review of U.S. history is more meaningful than another recitation of facts — not because we have not heard it before, but because it forces us to look at these historical realities in a new light. That part of the book comprises the first five chapters.

As you arrive at Chapter Six, it's "exam time." Not for you as the reader, but you as a member of the community, as an individual, a force in the body politic, a contributor in the productive engine of society. He asks: Is America in Decline? If you think you know the answer, you'd better read this chapter again. We must understand this question, and how dangerous a distraction it is, before our journey continues.

Chapter Seven is the report card, the diagnosis, the analysis of the patient's condition and prospects. Many people thriving in Washington today, and most of the nation's media, persist in making Washington and Congress the center of the governing universe. As children of the '60s and '70s, their attitude is understandable — but useless for the 21st Century.

The good news about this book is that, despite two decades of government service, Wishard does not indulge that fantasy. He recognizes our form of government as a product of our people, not as the engineer of our people. Government is more the mirror, and less the artist. Just as the Founding Fathers started with "We The People," Wishard knows to stay in that mode.

But, for that very reason, Members of Congress may get more out of this book than almost any other participant in our society.

The final chapter may be the most important. Wishard brings us face-to-face with the assumptions we must address before confronting the 21st Century. Ignore these questions, and we may, or may not, survive the new millennium.

But heed this warning: Even if you know your U.S. history, you can't simply jump to the final assumptions about our nation that must be revisited. You've got to accept or reject the road to the challenge. It is the very act of attitudinally accepting or rejecting this description of our past that makes possible the defining of our future.

Wishard's *American Future* is about our individual and collective journey. If we had a Thomas Jefferson, James Madison or a George Mason, Van Wishard might pale in comparison. Because we don't, he doesn't. He realizes this, and has stated as much in other venues; so he has bravely stepped up to the plate.

Yet, somewhere among us are the founding fathers and mothers of the 21st Century, America's third century as a society. They will answer the questions posed by Wishard either by affirmative mental exercises or by default. The latter approach is fraught with danger — for to default is to just let things happen. That should send a shudder through anyone so foolish or fortunate as to serve in the U. S. Congress.

The one assumption Wishard does not consider is the one that assumes current governmental structures to be sufficient for future needs. But maybe he is right not to tackle this point. Because, up until recently, all government-sector players have been servants of the people. Therefore, this issue really should not be addressed to the governing class.

Instead, we the governed must answer the question and then tell, or force, the servants to do what we want done. Unless, of course, we wish to abandon our old assumption that this government is the tool of the governed.

But, even if we want to make that decision, we should make it, rather than let it happen by default. We, not those who are operating governments, should decide on the structure of government. If we can better survive the third American century by adopting the Greek system (random drawings to select representatives), or if we prefer a parliamentary system, a high-tech instantaneous democracy, or the republic we already have, then let us eventually decide.

Jerome F. Climer
June 1992

INTRODUCTION

Power seemed to have outgrown its certitude and to have asserted its freedom... At the rate of progress since 1800, every American who lived into the year 2000 would know how to control unlimited power. He would think in complexities unimaginable to an earlier mind.

Henry Adams, 1905

You and I are living in the midst of the most difficult period America has ever known — more difficult than World War II, the Depression or even the Civil War. For America is at the center of a global cyclone of change, a change so vast and deep that it is difficult to encompass it as we pursue our daily routine.

We can stand at the bottom of the Grand Canyon, pull a hand-held telephone out of our shirt pocket, and call Paris. A mother can carry the fertilized ovum of her daughter in her womb, and give birth to a baby who is simultaneously her child and her grandchild. Soon we shall be able to determine some of that child's characteristics. We are redefining the respective roles of men and women, roles that had been accepted in most cultures throughout history. We can stand on the Moon, literally move mountains, or build new structures atom by atom. Adams was right: We have achieved all power.

And, in achieving this power, we redefine our understanding of reality. This redefinition reaches into the very core of the human psyche.

Such profound change causes us to experience mass confusion about everything — about the economy, about education, about values, about sexual roles, about the function of a family, about the source of authority, about the role of the State, about the real meaning and content of love, about the wellsprings of freedom, about the existence of God — indeed about the very meaning of life.

Understandings clear to our ancestors over the centuries are no longer clear to us because, due to these mind-bending changes, we are experiencing reality in a new way.

It's a time of incomparable trial. We are asked to do what no other people in history has done: To absorb and assimilate more change than took place in all history prior to the modern era, and to incorporate those changes into a new expression of individual existence and collective purpose. Our forbears had centuries or generations to adapt to change; we have only decades.

This time of trial is also the greatest opening up of vistas and new possibilities the world has ever known. For us to imagine the possibilities of the future is like asking the ancient Egyptians to imagine the age of computers, TV and space travel.

All of this change, and its introduction of new possibilities, alters existing habits of thought, patterns of life, established relationships and institutional arrangements. The feeling we have — that life is out of control — is but the process of one civilization, and one way of viewing life, yielding to a new civilization, and to the birth of a new understanding.

In light of such change, it is my wish that this book offers you a frame of reference for better assessing what's happening to America. It's not my intention to try to "solve" the many problems that confront us. Rather, I hope these pages encourage you to think more deeply about the American future than you have ever thought before.

Eric Hoffer once noted that America is the only country not built by a privileged class, but by the people. It is we — you and me — who are going to have to carry America forward to its next stage, its next expression of human dignity and liberty. I hope that what's written here offers some prompting that will better enable us to give birth to such an expression.

This book offers three broad perspectives. Chapters One through Three look at what has been the essence of the American experience. Chapters Four through

Seven consider the years between 1945 and today. The final chapter looks at some of the underlying assumptions that need to be revisited as we move into a new century, and a new millennium.

One last thought: The book is only a starting point, a groping forward for understanding. It is not all-encompassing; it's not complete; it does not offer the final word on America's future.

And therefore I would appreciate it if those of you who feel so inclined would write me your thoughts as a result of having read the book. If you would do that, then maybe, together, we can advance our effectiveness in bringing to birth the next phase of the American Experiment.

Wm. Van Dusen Wishard
1805 Wainwright Drive
Reston, VA 22090
TEL/FAX: (703) 437-9261

CHAPTER ONE

THE EXPERIMENT

I know of only three times in the western world when statesmen consciously took control of historic destinies: Periclean Athens, Rome under Augustus, and the founding of your American republic.

Alfred North Whitehead

America began — and continues today — as an Experiment; an experiment in people choosing to govern themselves, in a nation being shaped by ordinary people rather than by an elite, and in balancing the rights of the individual with the collective needs of society as a whole.

Such an experiment brought millions of people from almost every country on earth to live in America. In 1782, Hector St. John de Crevecoeur noted that in America "individuals of all nations are melted into a new race of men, whose labors and posterity will one day cause great changes in the world." Like many of his fellow Frenchmen,

Crevecoeur had come to explore the possibilities of this new continent America. "The American," he wrote, "is a new man, who acts upon new principles; he must therefore entertain new ideas and form new opinions."[1]

The story of America — the first colonial people to declare their independence from a European country — is the drama of these new "Americans" putting into practice those new principles, entertaining those new ideas and acting on those new opinions.

The results are known the world over: The Declaration of Independence, with its emphasis on equality, natural rights and government by the consent of the governed; the Constitution, which demonstrated how a central government could respect the sovereignty of its States and yet derive its sanction and power directly from the body of the people; the Bill of Rights, which guaranteed the rights of each citizen.

Mindful of Europe's religious wars, this country's founders explicitly designed an order which emphasized separation of Church and State. At the same time, they recognized the inextricable link between liberty and belief in a Supreme Being. "Of all the dispositions and habits which lead to political prosperity," President Washington advised Congress, "religion and morality are indispensable supports, [so] let us with caution indulge the supposition that morality can be maintained without religion."[2]

Thomas Jefferson, the American who most represented the 18th-century Enlightenment, asked whether "the liberties of a nation can be thought secure when we have removed their only firm basis, a conviction in the minds of the people that these liberties are the gifts of God?"[3] Jefferson's feelings about Christ were such that he extracted all Christ's words from the Bible, and published them in a separate volume, which became known as *The Jefferson Bible*.

Such was the foundation of America, established within a dozen years at the close of the eighteenth century, just as the French began to detonate their ancient structure of monarchy.

The first part of the 19th century saw American expansion Westward, as well as the beginning of industrialization. By 1830, one-third of the American people lived west of the Appalachian Mountain range which had been the Western border of the original 13 colonies. Eli Whitney, who had manufactured muskets for the government during the Revolutionary War, conceived the idea of having one worker make only one part of a machine, and having all parts be interchangeable. Thus was invented the basis of mass-production, a means of assembly which was to vastly lower costs.

During this time, three different parts of America began to take shape: The industrial North, the agricultural South, and a West that represented opportunity for anyone who would go claim and farm the land. People flooded in from all corners of

Europe. Between 1830 and 1850, about two-and-a-half million people crossed the Atlantic Ocean to become part of this new nation.[4] They were drawn not only by the promise of unlimited opportunity, but also by the absence of any legal class distinction such as had stratified European society. In America, absence of talent was the only barrier to bettering one's condition. Thus John Jacob Astor, an immigrant who came to America scarcely able to read or write, amassed a $20,000,000 fortune before he died in 1848.

The country's sheer size and the vastness of opportunity bred a sense of unlimited optimism that was to become an enduring trait of the American character. If Americans today sometimes seem simplistic in our optimism about what can be done to better the condition of mankind, it's in large measure thanks to the sense of endless possibility that is part of the legacy we inherited.

As the three sections of America took advantage of their respective natural endowments, vast differences in attitude and outlook developed. In particular, the inherent contradictions between an industrial North and an agricultural South festered and grew.

Those differences were wider than simply opposing opinions about the institution of Slavery, as critical as that was. Slavery had been a universal phenomenon. Starting in the 16th century, Arab slave-traders sold into bondage millions of Africans who ended up in Europe, India, the Middle East,

South and Central America as well as North America.

While Slavery lay at the core of the differences between America's North and South, it was by no means the only difference. The two portions of America were divided by other questions, such as whether an agrarian South could preserve its character or should be forced to conform to the industrial character of the North; whether the Southern planter should be forced to take his values and morality from the Northern businessman; indeed, a question of what would become of liberty if "Union" were to mean an enforced uniformity.

Such tensions, which had been present since the founding of America, finally erupted into what many historians have considered to be the defining event of American history. The Civil War cost more American lives than this country lost in all wars it fought in the 20th century. The war was fought, so President Lincoln said at Gettysburg, to determine whether a nation "conceived in liberty, and dedicated to the proposition that all men are created equal" can long endure.

America did endure — just — and in the process became one nation.

In the four decades following the Civil War, America reaped the benefits of its own Industrial Revolution, developed new industries, established a continental economy and emerged as a world economic and military power. A new class of leaders appeared —

financiers, businessmen, entrepreneurs — whose supreme value was the acquisition of wealth.

By 1890, the American "frontier" had disappeared, and the national work became one of consolidation rather than expansion. By this time, America had 63,000,000 people (60,000,000 more than when George Washington was President a century earlier), 160,000 miles of railroad and 3,000,000 square miles of contiguous territory without tariff barriers.[5] Railroads, coal, steel, oil, the electrical and chemical industries, were now the engines of economic growth. By the turn of the century, the automobile and telephone industries had emerged, and Americans owned 13,000 cars and just over one million telephones. J.P. Morgan formed the United States Steel Corporation, and the era of the "billion-dollar company" was at hand.[6]

A new America had emerged. In 1790, 90% of the population had been farmers. By 1890, farmers comprised only 30% of the population (today they are less than 3%).[7] Between 1875 and 1905, the gross national product quadrupled.[8] The new America brought with it the "mass society." Mass-production, mass communications, mass education, mass entertainment and mass consumption began to define the way America worked and lived.

The new American sentiment was summed up by the Washington *Post* in June 1896: "A new consciousness seems to have come upon us — consciousness of strength — and with it a new appetite, the yearning to show our strength...

Ambition, interest, land hunger, pride, the mere joy of fighting, whatever it may be, we are animated by a new sensation. We are face-to-face with a strange destiny."[9]

Key to developing this new era was the integration of applied science and business, perhaps best typified by Thomas Edison. Edison, who may have affected 20th-century America as much as any other individual, had more than 1,000 patents to his credit, on which whole industries have been built. He was part of a new breed who moved America from agricultural beginnings to industrial might.

CHAPTER TWO

HARBINGERS OF CHANGE

Nothing endures but change.

Heraclitus

Before we leave this period of American life, it is worthwhile to comment on the subtle changes in attitudes and public ethos that had been taking place beneath the surface.

Culturally, intellectually and spiritually, early America was an extension of Europe, especially Great Britain, France and Germany. The people who settled Massachusetts, Maryland and Virginia were all raised in the Judeo-Christian tradition; they were cultural descendants of Dante, Shakespeare, Milton, Bach, and Handel. In this sense, spiritual and cultural values were paramount and, along with the themes of the Enlightenment, formed the basis of America's founding beliefs. Material benefits were meant to raise the individual to a higher cultural and spiritual plane.

In the minds of many, the lush vastness and beauty of the primeval American wilderness gave rise to the hope of a deeper spiritual quality, based not on ecclesiastical dogma, but on the innate relationship between man and nature. Crevecoeur, Jefferson, Cooper, Melville, Thoreau and Emerson all saw the possibility of this majestic wilderness, with its primal beauty and awe, producing a human being of higher spiritual sensitivity — someone that Old Europe, with its encrusted sophistication, could no longer produce.

As more Americans moved westward in the nineteenth century, however, this view of the potential of the American wilderness clashed with another view — the wilderness as a source of material development. Vast fortunes were there to be made in land, cattle, grain, timber and minerals. The wilderness was there to be exploited and used, because empires needed to be built.

So the earlier hopes of Jefferson, Emerson and like minds faded. The accumulation of wealth became an end in itself, as well as the measure by which man and his achievements were judged. The California Gold Rush of 1849 became the symbol of the outpouring of Earth's riches. Indeed, the very word rush denoted a nation in a hurry, and the energies of America accelerated in pursuit of instant fortune.

As author Frederick Jackson Turner noted, "America no longer seemed 'Nature's nation'... [T]he wild lands had been pillaged of their resources, and the nation had derived purely economic benefits therefrom."[10] The moral and spiritual benefits that some had supposed would accrue to America from its wild lands had not been realized, and "Americans in 1875 appeared, if anything, more estranged from nature and from their lands than their counterparts in the Old World."[11] Observant Europeans even began to comment about America, as did Germany's Count Keyserling, that "one rarely hears of any other standard of value but that of quantitative achievement."[12]

Turner goes on to note that "the machine" may have been the truest expression of the American genius. But the question still had to be asked whether the machine, and a machine-oriented culture, could produce those "moral and spiritual blessings that were the ultimate promise of American life."[13] While the taming of the American continent and the raising of great metropolitan areas was one of the monumental technical achievements of all history, a price was eventually paid — in terms of America's own sense of its higher self, as well as the nation's relationship to, and stewardship of, the land and nature.

Thus it was that in his Inaugural Address to America in 1913, President Woodrow Wilson would say: "We see in many things that life is very great... But the evil has come with the good, and much fine gold has been corroded." Wilson talked of resources being "squandered." "There has been something crude and heartless and unfeeling in our haste to succeed and be great," Wilson cautioned. "Our thought has been 'Let every man look out for himself, let every generation look out for itself...'"

Sensing the dramatic transition taking place in American life, Wilson concluded: "We know our task to be no mere task of politics, but a task which shall search us through, whether we be able to understand our time and the need of our people..."[14]

Sixteen years later, Walter Lippmann, one of the great journalist/philosophers of 20th-century America, took Wilson's theme further. Lippmann saw the "acids of modernity" eating away at the base of the belief that had nourished the American experiment. Americans were a people composed of individuals who had lost association with their old landmarks.

"The religious synthesis has dissolved," he wrote in 1929. "The modern man no longer holds a belief about the universe which sustains a pervasive emotion about his destiny; he no longer believes genuinely in any idea which organizes his interests within the framework of a cosmic order." Lippmann saw Americans as people whose lives were an expression of "mere restlessness and compulsion, rather than conduct lighted by luminous beliefs."[15]

Such were the concerns of many of America's more thoughtful citizens in the early part of this century. These expressions are noted here because they represent a shift of emphasis in the American Experiment. The original 18th-century note of optimism and innocence began to be tinged with an awareness of the barrenness of material progress whenever that material progress is devoid of some deeper sustaining conviction. It is necessary to evaluate the assessments of men like Lippmann if we're to comprehend what formed the underlying realities of America in the 1990s.

CHAPTER THREE

ENTERING THE MODERN AGE

The American Century.

Henry Luce

The first half of the 20th century held three successive tasks for America: (a) Becoming a world power, (b) building a mass consumer society, and (c) coping with the Depression.

America's late entry into the First World War (1917) partially explains why the war was not such a disillusioning catastrophe for America as it was for Great Britain and France. In fact, some argue that the real significance of America's participation in the First World War lay not in the war itself, but in the fact that, after 300 years of withdrawal from the "Old World" (as Americans affectionately called Europe), America reversed the flow and re-entered the Old World. This was perhaps best symbolized by the fact that Woodrow Wilson was the first American President, while in office, to travel to Europe.

The First World War had other consequences for America. It produced our first major experience with centralized control of economic resources. Minimal government interference in business and economic affairs had been one of the great factors encouraging economic development of the vast land mass of the United States. With the First World War came the need to establish priority use of America's resources, and with that came creation of the War Industries Board, the War Labor Policies Board and a host of bureaucracies in Washington. This was a watershed, for America never really returned to its prewar *laissez-faire* identity.

Robert Nisbet, one of America's leading sociologists, suggests that World War I gave birth to the present age in American history. The Great War, he argues, was the setting for America's entry into modernity — economic, political, social and cultural. "By 1920 the country had passed, within a mere three years, from the pre-modern to the distinctly and ineffaceably modern. Gone forever now the age of American innocence."[16]

America's rise to pre-eminent world economic and military power was another major outcome of the war. Great Britain and France both lost a generation of leadership. Germany lost an empire and faced ruinous debt. Russia was in revolutionary turmoil. And Japan, despite giant strides achieved since 1868 and the acquisition of Germany's Pacific territories, was still in the early stages of industrialization.

So, despite the unforeseen depression to come, America stood alone in terms of economic and military strength — a position that would not be challenged for over half a century.

The Great Depression, which saw every fourth American without a job, left psychological scars that shaped attitudes for decades. In much the same way as the Japanese who lived through the rebuilding of Japan after World War II held an economic outlook different from those who've grown up in a more prosperous Japan, the Americans who lived through the Depression embodied certain attitudes of thrift, saving, life-as-more-than-consumption which are not so prevalent today. While the trough of the Depression was hit in the early 1930s, by 1940 America still had not fully recovered; only World War II finally ended the Great Depression for America.

Tomes have been written about the Second World War, and television has vividly brought movies depicting its horrors into our living rooms. So there is little need to dwell on the war here.

Wars, however, alter nations in fundamental ways, ways that are not always evaluated until decades later. It's not only a question of lost lives and destroyed physical assets. War summons forth great energies; some would even say the highest energies a people are capable of achieving. Thus, after all great wars there is a psychological release, a relaxation of effort, a decrease in authority, of religious beliefs and moral values. People think differently about life after experiencing war's carnage and slaughter. Human purposes, values and mores all undergo change.

Emerson had seen this clearly after the Civil War. "We hoped," he wrote, "that in peace, after such a war, a great expansion would follow in the mind of the country; grand views in every direction — true freedom in politics, in religion, in social science, in thought. But the energy of the nation seems to have expended itself in the war."[17]

And so it was with America, despite her ascendency to the pinnacle of world power after the Second World War. The effects of the war on Americans, and on what had been considered the unwritten American ethos, were to be a primary influence on America throughout the second half of the 20th century.

CHAPTER FOUR

AMERICA AND THE 1950s: A WATERSHED

And now came the turning point, 1956:
The end of the British Empire and
the end of the rise of the American one.

John Lukacs

Theodore White once observed that Americans measure history in terms of decades — the "twenties," the "fifties," the "eighties." Europeans measure history in terms of Ages — the "Victorian Age" in England, *La Belle Epoque* in France, the "Weimar Republic" in Germany.[18] He might have added that Asians tend to measure history in terms of centuries — the "Han Dynasty" in China, or the "Heian Period" in Japan.

So it is that conventional wisdom presents the 1950s as the apex of the American Experience: An economically explosive but politically tranquil period ruled over by a passive and benevolent President Dwight Eisenhower.

Closer examination, however, reveals the 1950s as the end of the initial phase of the American Experiment, and the start of a new period.

For the first 175 years of its existence, America had a clear — if unstated — national purpose: To build a nation. By the 1950s, that task was essentially complete. While perfection of nationhood is a never-ending process, by the 1950s America had settled a continent; built a physical, legal, commercial and political infrastructure; fought a war to preserve Union; established the institutions to service a continental existence; secured her place as a world power; and placed herself at the forefront of world economic and technological advance.

What America needed by 1950 was to evaluate her condition, not only in terms of post-war circumstances, but also in light of her long-term trajectory as a cooperative enterprise. It was not simply a matter, now that the war was won, of getting on with life as normal. The need was to foresee the emergent age; to gain historical perspective which could offer insight on the American Experiment; and perhaps suggest a fresh direction and purpose relevant to the long-term technological/cultural/spiritual upheaval that had been transforming America and the world for at least a century.

No such reevaluation was undertaken, nor was any fresh sense of purpose put forth.

Indeed, few people even realized the juncture at which America stood. One who did was Adlai

Stevenson, twice a presidential nominee. Asked Stevenson in 1954: "Are America's problems but surface symptoms of something even deeper; of a moral and human crisis in the Western world which might even be compared to the fourth, fifth and sixth-century crisis when the Roman Empire was transformed into feudalism and primitive Christianity... Are we passing through one of the great crises of history when man must make another mighty choice?"[19]

In 1952, only seven years after the greatest military triumph in history, and two years into the decade that some people have considered the summit of the American experiment, Rollo May, a distinguished psychologist, wrote that the "chief problem of people in the middle decade of the 20th century is emptiness." This emptiness, May said, "has now moved from a state of boredom to a state of futility and despair which holds promise of dangers."[20]

Lewis Mumford, a renowned social commentator of the times, told America that "we stand on the brink of a new age: the age of an open world..." Mumford spoke to the heart of the crisis of which May and Stevenson had warned. "The difficulty is," Mumford wrote, "that our machine technology and our scientific methodology have reached a high pitch of perfection at a moment when other important parts of our culture, particularly those that shape the human personality — religion, ethics, education, the arts — have become inoperative or, rather, share in the general disintegration and help to widen it."[21]

But the Americans of the 1950s were too busy savoring victory's fruits, and reinventing a more superficial America, to consider Stevenson's or Mumford's assessments. America after World War II was not interested in ultimate ends; she was absorbed with immediate means. There was no time to pick up the threads of Lippmann's "luminous beliefs" or to explore the significance of May's insights. The 1950s became a transforming decade for America, a period when aggressive materialism shaped both perception and reality.

The consumption ethic did not suddenly emerge in the 1950s. America's Consumer Society had been launched in the 1890s. In 1899, economist Thorsten Veblen published *The Theory of The Leisure Class* in which he coined the phrase "conspicuous consumption" to describe American habits.

By the 1920s, the Consumer Society was taking giant strides with the introduction of cars, refrigerators, radios, electric washing machines and countless other conveniences which were touted as neces- sities by a newly born public relations industry.

Delayed by the Great Depression and World War II, the Consumer Society burst forth with all its pent-up power in the 1950s. Economic growth became an end in itself. The "consumer society" became the "throwaway society," and "planned obsolescence" was the order of the day. "Credit cards" were introduced and, in a four-year period, consumer credit ballooned 56%.[22] During the '50s, America's Gross National Product almost doubled; the Dow

Jones industrial Average virtually tripled; and individual share-owners jumped from six to 17 million.[23]

For the first time, the majority of workers were not engaged in tangible production, but in administration and services. The computer industry was born; machines could compute in ways and at speeds beyond human capability — a milestone in human history.

Another milestone was the creation of the model of the molecular structure of DNA. The possibility of genetic engineering was now at hand. Humans could now, in part, control evolution.

In 1954, the Supreme Court of the United States outlawed segregation by race in all American public schools. Three years later, President Eisenhower sent federal troops into Little Rock, Arkansas, to enforce the new law. In the following decade, Blacks would make more progress than in the 90 years that followed the Civil War.

In 1957, America entered the Space Age as the Soviets launched *Sputnik I.* Two years later Russia's *Lutnik III* sent back to Earth the first pictures ever taken of the far side of the moon. The Space Race was on, and America's reaction was one of virtual panic.

U.S. industrial competitiveness met its first serious post-war challenge in the 1950s. Volkswagen replaced Ford as the "world car" and, in 1956, for the first time, America imported more cars than we exported. Nineteen fifty-five was the last year that inflation actually declined in America. Since then, it has done nothing but rise, at varying rates.

The development of suburbia created the nuclear family, diminished the extended family and forever altered the structure of family life on which America had been built. The 1950s produced the first TV generation, causing our children to be raised in a different context, with wider horizons at earlier ages, than any prior generation.

Completely unnoticed was a change in the function of the American university. From inception, its purpose had been teaching, with research as a subordinate activity. The 1950s solidified a reversal of these functions. Research became the primary focus of America's major universities, with teaching relegated to a secondary position, frequently attended to by a graduate student.

The H-bomb was invented, and the world's first generation to grow up under the threat of possible extinction of the human species wrestled with new psychological pressures.

The moral ethos of America radically shifted during the 1950s. Who knows how many of the millions of veterans of World War II, having experienced the ultimate life-and-death challenge of war, abandoned previous attitudes toward sex, loosening the bonds of family cohesion? Invention of the "pill" accelerated the change in mores. All this was exemplified by the publication of *Playboy*, a magazine that never could have found a mass readership in an earlier America.

The character and purpose of culture changed in the 1950s. Sartre, Beckett, Camus and the "School of the Absurd" became dominant in philosophy, literature and cinema. "Life is a tale, told by an idiot, full of sound and fury, signifying nothing"[24] became the theme of cultural life. The "hero," represented by Jimmy Stewart or Gary Cooper, was replaced by the "anti-hero" as seen in James Dean or Marlon Brando.

The birth of "Rock" music in the 1950s was part of this cultural shift. Rock's underlying themes were exploitation of sex and rebellion. Neither of these were new themes, but to have them become the driving impulse of the culture was a clear break with the tradition of mainstream American music. (One recalls Plato's comment from *The Republic:* "A change to a new type of music is something to beware of as a hazard of all our fortunes. For the modes of music are never disturbed without unsettling of the most fundamental political and social conventions.")

Perhaps as a symbol of all this change, Sunday lost priority acceptance as the day of spiritual renewal and worship, and became just another day at the shopping mall. In fact, in 1954, America discovered the mall.

In sum, the 1950s were a watershed in American life; and it is for that reason that this narrative dwells more on the '50s than on other periods which could be perceived as more dramatic. It was this sea-change in American life and mores that set the stage for 1960s turbulence. But, at the time, few people realized what has taking shape.

Americans didn't see what had happened for many reasons, not least of which was that our attention was focused on Berlin, Quemoy, Matsu, Budapest, Kerela, Bandung, Guatemala, Lebanon, Peking, Suez and Tokyo. The struggle to rebuild war-ravaged Europe and Japan, to construct a postwar world economic and trade structure, to contain Soviet imperialism and to assist newly inde- pendent nations absorbed the full energies of the nation. The role of world leader was a new role for America, especially when one considers that, only two decades earlier, isolationism was embedded in the American psyche.

In this sense, America did not choose her role after World War II and during the 1950s; it was thrust upon her. The acceptance of that role was not part of a considered plan in the next stage of America's development as a country. Rather, America was the only nation capable of responding to the mounting emergencies. And respond she did — as best she could — with the Marshall Plan, the Truman Doctrine, the formation of NATO, the defense of South Korea, the reconstruction of Japan and the creation of a world trade structure.

But the enormous responsibility of this involvement meant that America did not have the time, or did not take the time, to evaluate her own growth path as a nation, and to determine the best course for her future.

Few realized how America had come to the end of a critical phase in her own development; that the coming decades needed to be built on a vision and conception every bit as daring as was that of those who had launched the initial phase of the American Experiment. Few recognized, as did Stevenson, that America had arrived at a point where "man must make another mighty choice."

So the choice, at least in terms of long-term direction, was not made. Instead, consumer demand, pent-up during the war, exploded, and a tidal wave of new technology — from xerography to DDT to jet-powered planes — washed across America. Wartime research and development generated a period of technological change not equalled in scope perhaps "since the adoption of farming some 10,000 years earlier."[25] The "affluent society," so America was told, had arrived.

CHAPTER FIVE

THE SIXTIES AND BEYOND

The schism in the body social is a collective experience... Its significance lies in its being the outward and visible sign of an inward and spiritual rift.

Arnold J. Toynbee

Sensing that America was being carried forward by momentum rather than by any self-generated vision, John F. Kennedy tried to sound a note of higher calling. But even before his assassination, politics as public theater had begun to gain the upper hand over statesmanship, and the President's summons carried a diminishing clarity.

For Americans, the 1960s started with exhilarating hopes and ended with smashed dreams. The 1950s had been the high-water mark of "the American Way of Life." America had entered a new era, but the traditional Eastern establishment stood mute, offering little direction or vision. The 1960s, so many Americans thought, would wash away the wreckage of a collapsed order and remake America in the image of John and Bobby Kennedy and Martin Luther King. Events decided otherwise.

Despite the high hopes, the soaring rhetoric and even passage of the historic 1964 Civil Rights Act, there was no Jefferson, no Lincoln, not even a Wilson to turn to. Rachel Carson pricked America's bubble of technological bliss with publication of *Silent Spring*, launching the environmental movement; and Ralph Nader gave birth to the consumer movement with publication of *Unsafe At Any Speed*. "Free speech," the Beatles, grass, Woodstock and Chicago all became symbols for a generation.

The dominant concern of the second half of the '60s, however, was Vietnam, and it was left to America's "best and brightest" to take the country through its most soul-searching decade of the 20th century. Landing on the Moon in 1969, one of history's greatest triumphs of the human spirit, was momentarily exhilarating. But it could not provide the underlying sense of national direction that was lacking.

As an attempt to escape the frustrations of the '60s, the 1970s turned out to be even more of a marking decade. Crises in three areas brought America face to face with the end of the American Century. In 1971 America closed the gold window and devalued the dollar. Then the 1973 oil embargo and price quadrupling suddenly made our people aware that we were no longer in sole control of our economic destiny. Watergate and the resignation of President

Richard Nixon deepened agonizing doubts about America's capacity for effective self-government. In 1975 the Vietnam war closed as Americans were lifted by helicopter off the top of the U.S. embassy in Saigon, perhaps the worst humiliation since the capitol was burned by the British in 1812.

Double-digit inflation and oil-price hikes during 1973-74, and again in 1979-81, only confirmed what Americans intuitively knew, but were reluctant to admit: American world economic, military and political predominance came to an end in the 1970s.

The 1980s were a decade of America deciding whether to come to grips with the essential fact that the world had unalterably changed, and that new power centers had emerged. The question, inevitably, was no longer whether America was "Number One" (as a million bumper stickers proclaimed), but rather, in light of radically different global conditions, how to define the new American role and purpose.

The struggle with this reality was the undercurrent of the 1980s. It was reflected in three primary areas. Politically, Ronald Reagan promised to restore a lost glory, to reach back for the greatness of a bygone era and superimpose it on the present. "America is back!" was one theme of Reagan's 1984 presidential campaign. This reassuring theme assuaged the psyche of a distraught nation.

Culturally, the "nostalgia industry" sprang out of nowhere, bringing back 1950s musicals, old-time

Humphrey Bogart movies, 19th-century architecture and anything else that harked back to a simpler era of American life. Spiritually, the "born-again" movement captured millions of souls, and fundamentalism made a new presence for itself in both the spiritual and political life of the nation.

Coupled with this was a decade of strong economic growth and mind-bending technological development. The FAX machine sent letters zapping around the world in seconds, severely crimping the service of companies like Federal Express, which themselves had succeeded in displacing the old-style "Special Delivery" of the U.S. Mail.

Computer speeds multiplied to such an extent that time — calculations in trillionths of a second — became divorced from human comprehension. Superconductivity introduced technical possibilities heretofore seen only in science-fiction novels. And *nanotechnology,* the construction of new materials atom by atom, was hailed as the most significant technological advance of the 20th century.

Despite such technological advances, by the end of the '80s, the ersatz glory refurbished by the Reagan Presidency was a distant mist. Old doubts returned. Even while President Bush enjoyed unusually high public opinion approval, the question of *Quo Vadis, America?* dominated newspaper editorials, prestigious think-tank seminars and learned academic treatises.

Then, in November 1989, the unthinkable happened: The Berlin Wall collapsed. Communism, that ultimate global evil of 70 years, was vanishing like a vapor.

If the American reaction of "We've won! We've won the Cold War!" was simplistic, it was understandable. For 45 years, America had stood against the indescribable tyranny of Communism in all its guises. Billions of dollars, millions of tons of material and thousands of American lives had been spent so that people in far-off lands might remain free of the grip of the most all-encompassing totalitarianism the world has ever known.

Each American taxpayer had given thousands of dollars to feed, house and maintain the freedom of people he would never meet in a land he would never visit. Part of the national cost of this four decade-long outpouring of talent and treasure was America's loss of undisputed world economic and technological leadership.

But the end of the Cold War only exacerbated America's inner confusion about its direction. For 45 years, containing the Soviet Union had been the centerpiece of American foreign policy. Now what?

On August 2, 1990, "now what?" was temporarily answered as Iraq invaded Kuwait. America's need for clarity — "good guys" versus "bad guys" — was more than met in Saddam Hussein's monstrous crushing of Kuwait. For one brief shining moment, America surmounted deeper doubts about her destiny, summoned her allies, and gave herself to a cause of potential sacrifice and certain generosity.

But with the victory parades over, and the aura of high achievement evaporated, old doubts and uncertainty returned.

CHAPTER SIX

IS AMERICA IN DECLINE?

Mao Tse Tung, when asked his views on the effects of the French Revolution: "It's too soon to tell."

Richard Nixon

One of the contradictions of the past two decades is that, despite the record economic growth and avalanche of technology, the question has been constantly asked, "Is America in decline?"

Has America followed the path of Rome, Spain, France, Great Britain and all great powers which have had their day of glory, lost their greatness and subsequently become just one more nation?

In America, an entire industry has grown up drawing its sustenance debating this question. Would-be Oswald Spenglers, academics of all stripes, think tanks, public-policy journals as well as a few psychohistorians have all joined in the debate, some making small fortunes off their offerings.

It's a fair question — discussed not only in America, but also in government councils in Tokyo, Moscow, London, Bonn and probably every other capital of any consequence.

Decline, of course, is a relative condition, not easily given to quantification. Joseph S. Nye Jr. notes that scholars have advanced more than 200 causes for the decline of Rome, and they still disagree on dates.[26] Decline compared to what, and when?

Ample evidence exists to support the "America in decline" thesis.

By the mid-1970s, America had virtually lost its consumer-electronics industry. Indeed, General Electric Co. simply gave up competing with Japan in some consumer electronic products. America's need for help in financing military operations in Iraq could be interpreted as an example of "imperial overstretch." Japan has replaced America as the greatest source of finance capital, another indication that would seem to support the notion of America's decline. Japan is also the greatest donor of foreign aid, a position America held for three decades after World War II.

Not only has America lost market-share in industries such as automobiles where she had traditionally led, but America has lost whole industries as well. Machine-tools, VCRs, industrial ceramics, copiers and semiconductors are only a few of the industries where America has surrendered leadership to Japan.

Many portions of America's highways, bridges, sewer systems and inner cities are in a state of collapse. The ability of some of the country's major corporations to produce world-class quality products is not what it was three decades ago. Our high-school students perform abysmally on international academic tests, and even Harvard University finds that the reading comprehension of its students has declined significantly from levels of 70 years ago.

Congress's inability to manage government finances responsibly suggests a decline in the capacity of America's leaders to determine national priorities. In an average day, the national debt increases by over $1 billion, and $80 million is paid to foreign creditors in interest on the debt. Drugs, crime and the American family's condition also support the notion of national decline.

So, for those who want to argue the case of "America in decline," there is no lack of evidence that would seem to support their premise.

The "America in decline" thesis has a certain intellectual appeal, and it is in keeping with the great themes of Gibbon and Spengler, and with the speculations of Arnold Toynbee. Moreover, it resonates with the disenchantment and repudiation that entered American literature in the post-World War I period, and that, during the 1970s-80s, evolved into the nihilism predicted by Nietzsche a century earlier.

Evidence of the "declinists" notwithstanding, an army of voices denounces the theory of decline. Yes, these voices admit, a vast array of problems confronts America. But such problems do not automatically equate with decline. Such voices marshall their own evidence.

America produces roughly 23% of the gross world product, a figure that has held constant for the past 25 years. The U.S. economy in 1988 produced 45% of the total OECD economy.[27] During the 1980s, America created over 18 million jobs,[28] and averaged the start-up of over 250,000 new businesses each year.[29] During the same time, 14,000 new computer-software firms were started, and the number of software engineers increased about 28% a year.[30] As a share of gross national product, America's manufacturing sector continues to contribute in the low 20% range, much the same as it has since the 1960s.[31] In 1990, U.S. companies commanded nearly 70% of world computer revenues.[32]

Gauged by purchasing power, Americans are the most prosperous people in the world, with an estimated per-capita purchasing-power parity $4,000 above the Japanese and $3,000 above the Germans.[33] By most economic measures, the bottom fifth of American families live better than the average of Japanese families.[34] Although the largest banks in the world are Japanese, America dominates the list of the world's most profitable banks. Many of America's pummeled industries have rebounded, and Japanese firms now actually import specialty steels from the United States.

America's education has serious problems, but its higher education is good enough for over 360,000 foreign students to flock to American universities each year. Both the high-school dropout and illiteracy rates are at an all-time low.

Ninety-six percent of all Americans say they are very proud of their country, while only 59% in Germany and 62% in Japan express a similar degree of national pride.[35] In America, 71% of the people believe they have a good chance of improving their standard of living, while in Australia only 58% have the same belief, and in Germany less than 36% of the people hold such a hope.[36]

Countless public-opinion polls show that most Americans are willing to make sacrifices. Sixty-one percent of the people are willing to pay at least 10% more in taxes if the new revenue is used to address national problems.[37] Voluntarism is at an all-time high in such areas as drug-rehabilitation, school-improvement, environmental clean-up, and in helping the homeless. The dominant majority of Americans of all ethnic backgrounds want to be part of something bigger and better — something greater than just themselves.

Perhaps the most compelling argument of the "anti-declinists" is that, in their view, the American concept of democracy and free markets are being put in place by most governments around the world.

So what do all the arguments — for or against — "the decline of America" theory prove? Nothing. Absolutely nothing — except, perhaps, how a nation can be diverted from considering the core questions of its future.

The "America in decline" debate is based on a reading of the historic trajectories of great empires such as Greece, Rome, France and England. After each empire's hour of glory had faded, some new nation would rise to replace it as the dominant power of the new time.

But those historic evolutions took place in the age of the nation-state, when individual national development rates had their separate organic rhythm, and when communications between nations was relatively slow. (It took 12 days for the news of Abraham Lincoln's assassination to reach London.) The world no longer lives in such an age. Instant communications and jet travel have foreshortened time and distance, and they have linked all people together in some configuration of a world community. The existence of this global community is the dominant reality of our time.

It is unlikely that ever again the world will see one nation exercise the hegemonic power enjoyed by Great Britain in the 18th-19th century, or by the United States in the 20th century. The rise of other power centers means the end of one nation dominating world affairs.

Speculation as to whether Japan will succeed America as "Number One" is as futile as it is irrelevant. Even if Japan were to surpass the United States in GNP, Japan (or any other country) could never duplicate past global roles played by America and Great Britain. Why not? Because the world has changed too much, with too many significant centers of economic and political power, for such a possibility to emerge.

So the question of whether America is in decline misleads us. It's a question framed by those whose worldview only looks backward at history. It is not a question of urgency to those who seek to understand the forces shaping the future of America and the world. In this sense, the "America in decline" syndrome is diverting us from far more essential considerations.

CHAPTER SEVEN

SO WHERE IS AMERICA?

As the most technologically advanced great nation in the late 20th century, we are a center from which radiate the forces that unify human experience.

Daniel J. Boorstin

If decline is not the relevant context within which to consider America, what is? Simply put, one form of civilization is yielding to a new form. This is a process global in scope and nature, and it's being led by America.

America is the midwife of the most profound technological, social, economic, cultural, spiritual transformation the world has known — certainly in the past 500 years, and possibly since the advent of the agricultural age. It is a transformation affecting every institution and assumption that has supported the American Experiment for 200 years. It is a transformation that affects society's entire structure. It's changing how Americans organize our affairs and how we relate to each other and to the world. More fundamentally, it is altering the individual's concept of self, and how that self relates to inner consciousness and global reality.

Such is the scope of change affecting not only America, but every nation, and at every level of life. The pace of this change, for a variety of reasons, moves at different speeds in different countries. Still, no nation on earth escapes its effects.

Japan, with its 2,000-year history, has developed a unique culture. Most of that time, Japan has been isolated from the intellectual currents of the other parts of the globe. Thus Japan has emerged with its culture more tightly woven into its daily life, and business activities, than is the case with any other industrial nation. This cultural cohesion gives Japan a certain degree of stability as the waves of change crash over the nation. Even so, Japan is not immune to the forces that have affected America over the past decade. Japan is changing, and that change is accelerating.

America, however, has nothing remotely approaching Japan's cultural cohesion and heritage. The purely American cultural heritage dates back to the 19th century's first decades. Prior to the 1850s, America drew its culture from Europe. But even then, that European cultural infusion was absorbed only by a minority of Americans. For the past 140 years, the overwhelming majority of Americans has been raised on the diet of a technically sophisticated culture, but one that lacked the spiritual depth of an earlier period.

On the one hand, such a condition permits the American to adapt quickly to new situations. Historically, change has been the normal state of affairs for most; this ability to adapt has been one of America's great strengths. At the same time, the absence of deep cultural roots leaves Americans more easily buffeted by the storms of change. Culture in its deepest and broadest sense is the seedbed of spiritual grounding and psychological stability. So a people with a shallow culture will be emotionally whipsawed by the lashes of change more easily than will those who have inculcated a culture of depth and cohesion.

Understanding this is essential to evaluating the American condition, as the very essence of culture is being shredded and reshaped. Every American is being bashed by external change, as well as uprooted internally by changes taking place within his own psyche. The sources and causes of these changes are many, and some have already been discussed. Yet certain primary causes of change need further mention.

<u>Urbanization</u>. Urbanization isn't uniquely American. However, it has had particular consequences for the American Experiment. America was founded as an agricultural society. By 1820, the first urban area of 100,000 people appeared. Today nearly 300 urban areas have populations of 100,000 or more.

Such movement of people from the land to the city was, of course, inevitable with industrialization. But the shift from an agricultural to an urban nation has perhaps been the basic change in American life, producing results Americans have neither fully evaluated nor known how to cope with.

Large cities have obviously been the generators of great commercial activity as well as artistic development. Serving as a focal point of intellectual ferment, cities the world over have been the home environment of great art and literature.

But when cities grow beyond a certain size, mass psychology predominates and the individual tends to lose his identity and sense of individual being. Personal values frequently become subsumed in mass attitudes. As a general rule, the moral temper of people living in large cities tends to be less clearly defined than those living in small towns or out in the country.

Commenting on this in 1946, Carl Jung wrote: "It is a notorious fact that the morality of society as a whole is in inverse ratio to its size; the greater the aggregation of individuals, the more the individual factors are blotted out, and with them morality, which depends entirely on the moral sense of the individual and on the freedom necessary for this."[38] Jung's diagnosis and treatment of patients led him to believe that the whole of life might be divided between a "city mind" and a "country mind."

As a consequence of this shift from an agricultural to an urban nation, of the move from the land to the city, a fundamental change in the relationship between the individual American and his natural environment took place. The American suddenly saw himself outside the domain of nature, no longer subject to its laws and cycles — in essence separating himself from nature, no longer to be fed or shaped by the life-sustaining elements of natural forces. Nature became something to be dominated, exploited and harnessed for industrial purposes.

While the easing of life's physical burdens through control of natural forces has been a seminal advance of the 20th century, this separation of the individual from nature generated psychological consequences which produced a different type of American from a century earlier. Once Americans cut ourselves off from our intimate relationship with the Earth and encased ourselves in the synthetic environment of the "concrete jungle," we were cut off from the very source of psychological and spiritual nourishment.

No longer did time have the same meaning as when the farmer knew how essential time was in the growth of his produce. No longer was there the same awareness of the change of seasons, and the realization of the distinct role each season plays in the cycle of life. No longer was there a sensitivity to life's organic process and a sense of each individual being part of it.

Instead, there were the new imperatives of urban life — accelerated tempo, collective existence, and an absorption in mechanical and bureaucratic processes. This had an inevitable psychological result — the inner "emptiness" Rollo May diagnosed in 1952. This separation of ourselves from nature is one source of the alienation, boredom, crime, psychological disorientation and social disruption plaguing America today.

However, over the past three decades, a recognition of what was lost has spread across America. Countless popular movements have risen in an attempt to bring America's life into equilibrium. In their narrowest definition, these movements have specific objectives such as saving the whales, or eliminating acid rain, or preserving California's redwood trees. In the broadest definition, these movements, knowingly or unknowingly, are attempts to reintegrate America's life back into nature's eternal order.

What is happening with these movements is far more than "environmental protection." Whether they are aware of it or not, their underlying impulse is to recapture the organic relationship between the individual and nature — a relationship that existed for millions of years before 1850 and America's Industrial Revolution.

Despite the reactions of Americans whose primary perspective is framed by economic-growth statistics, these movements, with all their obvious deficiencies, are hopeful indicators. If they mature, they could help take the American Experiment, indeed the dream of the human family, to its next stage of development.

Technology. New technology always changes human life in ways not anticipated.

When the first television system (in the form of the iconoscope) was developed in 1924, no one could have predicted that television would one day alter the character and quality of American politics, government, public information, education, entertainment, culture and religious worship. But that's what's happening.

One of America's leading authorities on television is Neil Postman, Professor of Communications at New York University. Professor Postman's analysis of what television is doing to America is worth quoting verbatim.

> With the emergence of modern communications media, mainly television, all serious public discourse has been transformed into show business or entertainment. Education, news, politics and even religion have been trivialized, losing their seriousness and dignity.
>
> In this mass-media culture dominated by television, everything is geared to pleasing the consumer. Yet, over the ages, the essential function of culture has not been to please, but to negotiate between what people want and what they need. Culture is about what the society and the individual need to survive into the future with their dignity intact. Culture is not about amusement, but about sustaining the acquisition of civilization.

> By the time the average American child even enters school, the working of his mind has been trained by watching some 5,000 hours of television. The most recent figures indicate that, by high school's end, that child will have watched nearly 20,000 hours. During that time, a child will see about one million commercials, making them our culture's chief source of socializing values. Not mom and dad, church or school, but Proctor and Gamble are transmitting the values which we all share.

In discussing the relationship between television and education, Professor Postman noted:

> The whole concept of education is based on delayed gratification and the hierarchy of prerequisites. Education is based on restraint and self-discipline. It is based on the importance of transmitting culture through language. Television culture is fundamentally hostile to that tradition.[39]

It was in the 1950s that television became a standard American household item. America is now moving into its fifth television decade.

Television is the most effective instrument ever invented for influencing the minds of masses of people. (It took 40 years for *Gone With The Wind* to sell 21 million copies. But, in one night, 55 million people watched the movie version.)[40] As *The Wall Street Journal* noted, "TV has become more significant than any other single factor in shaping the way most of us view our world ... more than religion or politics."[41]

According to some communications experts, television transformed the way we grow from childhood to adulthood, blurred traditional child/adult roles, loosened distinctions between male/female and public/private, altered ideas of gender behavior, changed our perceptions of political leaders, and dissipated established adherence to authority.[42]

Yet no serious attempt has ever been made, either by the television industry or by the U.S. government, to evaluate television in the terms Professor Postman describes, and to decide what might be done about it. It was simply a case of develop it, use it, and worry about the effects later. Commercial interests ruled.

So the question arises: What about other technologies? What about computers? In 1990, there were already 50 million personal computers in use in the United States.[43] We are fascinated by the incredible capacities and powers of the computer. But is America putting them into every office, schoolroom and home before really understanding what effect they have on the people who use them?

There are some indications that this may be the case. Research is showing that many computer users tend to think of their minds as machines, to see self in terms of mechanism rather than, as all religions have taught, in terms of meaning.

Children have always defined themselves by drawing contrasts with animals. Now, confronted by computers and computerized toys, many children see the computer as their nearest neighbor. Something similar is happening with adolescents: Many are struggling to find their identity not in relationship to their families, or to the world around them, but in relationship to video games, music videos and computers.[44]

Other studies show that, for married couples whose work entails heavy use of computers, conversations between husband and wife tend to be reduced to information exchanges as opposed to talk about personal feelings. Children who use computers in classrooms grow impatient with teachers and parents whose explanations are drawn out or too wordy. Impatience and expectation of perfection from spouse or child is increasing as an attitude of those whose work involves extensive use of computers. Computer operators internalize the computer's standards for speed, accuracy, perfection and yes or no answers. They show little patience for nuance or ambiguity, and none for error.[45]

Right now, it is possible to put 20 million transistors on a single chip the size of a person's thumbnail. By the end of the century, it will hold one billion. That is equal to the power of the processing units of 20 Cray-2 supercomputers, the most powerful in use today.

In light of these developments, it ought to be asked: Is America doing the same thing with computers as we did with television? Admitting the obvious benefits of computers, will America, two decades from now, discover that the computer has changed human life in undesirable ways? Ways that could have been avoided had more care and attention been given to understanding the effects of computers before blanketing the country with them?

Similar questions arise about genetic engineering. Has America's leadership and the public adequately evaluated the implications of the Human Genome Project — identifying and mapping all 50,000 to 100,000 genes and determining the sequence of the three billion code letters in human DNA? Some scientists say that such an undertaking, which would cost a minimum of $3 billion, could rival in scope both the Manhattan Project and the Apollo program, and may exceed them in importance. Is there a public consensus on the purpose and need of such a venture?

And don't forget nanotechnology — machines that control matter at the scale of molecules — placing every atom in structures ranging from small molecules to giant systems of human dimensions or larger.

The question arises not about technology *per se*, but about whether America has thought through the human purposes which alone can give adequate direction to its development and use. Technology developed simply for its own sake does not enhance human life and happiness. The more that rationalized technology — not based on meeting human needs and purposes — takes over our lives, the more irrational becomes the "product" technology is supposed to serve — people. Rationalized power and order, pushed to their ultimate limit, lead to their self-destructive inversion: Disorganization, subjective disorientation, mental aberration and violence.

The use of technology must be based on the ability of people to assimilate technology and convert it into a satisfying life. Technology developed simply for its own sake cannot enhance human life and happiness. Technology development must be integrated with some common affirmation of the underlying meanings that deepen and sustain human growth and, ultimately, the purpose of the human adventure.

Absent such definition, further technological development may only compound existing problems. America's space program, particularly Space Station *Freedom,* may be a case in point. Many people argue that what started as a stirring and heroic adventure on the cutting edge of science as well as the human spirit, has degenerated into a directionless bureaucratic engineering program. Does this reflect America's own lack of direction? Arthur C. Clarke, world-renowned author and the man who proposed using the geo-stationary orbit for communications satellites, noted: "America will not know where she's going in space until she decides where she's going in the world, what her mission is as a nation."[46]

Beyond this, the world may have entered a stage where certain scientific and technological projects are too large and expensive to be undertaken by one nation alone, and can no longer be justified by some outdated concept of national prestige. For example, should America be investing in the *Freedom* space station, or is it more to the point for America, Japan and Europe to consider jointly establishing a research facility on the Moon?

Besides considering such operational questions, America needs to reestablish a fundamental moral rationale for new technology. Technology, in and of itself, is not an expression of human purpose. It does not affirm any enduring value. It is an extension of means, not a definition of ends. The mission of technology should consist of enhancing human life and enabling people more fully to realize what it means to be human. Fulfilling this mission requires a rethinking of basic assumptions.

For over 100 years now, America has concentrated on the requirements of technological development — power, motion, uniformity and regularity and, more recently, miniaturization. But if technology is to enable people to realize more fully their potential as human beings, America will have to balance the needs of technology with the requirements of people developing their higher potential. This means greater emphasis on those agents that encourage individual wholeness, intuition, purpose, generosity and the impulse to higher reaches of being.

What gives human life its quality and meaning is the element of becoming, the very core of each individual's being. The emphasis must be on human growth, on life, on life's creative impulse of becoming. What do Americans as individuals seek to become? And what do we seek for America to become?

Only when these questions are answered will America know what technologies to develop and how best to use them. And only then will technology realize its full potential.

Universal Nation. Newspaper columnist Ben J. Wattenberg has written a book entitled *The First Universal Nation*. Wattenberg argues that the influx of immigrants from Asia, Latin America, Africa and the Moslem world infuses America with a fresh vitality and dynamism.

America historically is a nation of immigrants. But the origins and composition of that immigration are radically changing. Until 1960, about 80% of America's immigrants came from Europe. Since 1960, about 80% have come from places other than Europe.[47] Nearly one-fourth of America's immigrants are professional or technical workers who significantly strengthen America's work force.[48]

Wattenberg points to Dr. Ching-Wu Chu (the University of Houston physicist, born in China, who discovered high-temperature superconductivity) and to General Colin Powell (Chairman of the Joint Chiefs of Staff, whose mother came from

Jamaica) as prime examples of this new immigration which is giving America a fresh vigor as the world heads into the 21st century. This new immigration from places other than Europe will, according to Wattenberg, makes America the first "universal nation."

According to some estimates, by the middle of the next century, 50% of Americans will be made up of Blacks, Asians and Hispanics. During the 1980s, Los Angeles County's white non-Hispanic majority became a minority.[49] Florida's Dade County school system now includes students from 123 countries.[50] Stanford University has more minorities than Caucasians. Almost half of the 1990 Westinghouse Scholars were Asian-Americans.[51] In another eight years, every third child in New York's public schools will be a Black, Hispanic or Asian.[52] Over 7,200 Blacks hold elective office in America.[53] Given its number of Hispanics, Miami is now the northernmost city of Latin America. In Chicago, there are more Moslems than Methodists, and more Hindus than Presbyterians.[54]

When the Declaration of Independence was signed in 1776, the 56 signatories were white males, of European descent, and all from the Judeo-Christian tradition. Until the 1960s, when one spoke of an American, one was usually (and unfortunately) referring to someone of a European, Judeo-Christian heritage.

Within that European, Judeo-Christian heritage, however, there were many ethnic, cultural and religious differences. The majority of immigrants to the United States left many of these differences behind and were assimilated into "Americans." To a certain extent, America was a "melting pot" which took people of all conceivable backgrounds and sought to melt them into Crevecoeur's "new race of men."

This idea had varying degrees of success; but the whole point of America was not to preserve old differences; rather to create a new, distinctly American personality.

That no longer seems to be the case, at least in some quarters. The new view is one of a "multicultural" perspective where ethnic, sexual and cultural differences are emphasized. Group and ethnic interests are emerging as pre-eminent, and the very idea of a common culture is under assault. In a complete reversal of the historic idea of America, the degree of common ground seems to be shrinking. "If separatist tendencies go unchecked," writes Arthur Schlesinger, Jr., one of America's most prominent historians, "the result can only be the fragmentation, resegregation and tribalization of American life."[55]

The people of the United States are in the midst of redefining who they are and what an "American" really is. The consequences of this redefinition go right to the core of life, affecting education, culture and individual identity. It is likely that this redefinition will ultimately affect foreign policy as well.

In education, this redefinition centers on a fight over the school curriculum. Critics contend that courses on "Western Civilization" discriminate against people from non-Western traditions, and that contemporary Black or women authors should be included in courses in great literature along with Goethe, Dante and Shakespeare. In a dispute over curriculum at Stanford University, student demonstrators chanted, "Hey, hey, ho, ho, Western Culture's got to go."

Valid points are in contention here. Americans have been taught that Columbus "discovered" America in 1492, a notion which totally ignores the Native-Americans, their culture and history. Few U.S. history books include the creative role Blacks have played in the nation's development, and fewer still consider the history of Native-Americans as part of American history. So there is some essential need to reevaluate the history of the American experience.

At the same time, a nation dwelling primarily on its differences cannot survive. Nationhood grows out of what a people have in common. If multiculturalism is simply another means of asserting parochial interests over national interests, then it will only accelerate the fragmentation of America.

However, the fragmentation of America is representative of a deeper force at work all over the world. For centuries, people lived within their own ethnic and cultural boundaries. Sometimes those boundaries were between nations, sometimes such boundaries were formed by enclaves within nations. Living within a cultural boundary gave people a distinct sense of identity, of belonging to a clearly defined social unit. Myths and traditions interpreted the meanings of that culture and reinforced the sense of belonging.

Within a relatively short time, all those boundaries, to the extent they constitute the outer limits of a people's sense of identity, have been erased and a new boundary established. When the astronauts sent TV pictures of the Earth into millions of homes, schools and villages around the globe, man's view of who he is and to what cultural group he belongs was forever changed. All of a sudden, everyone saw themselves as part of one human community. It is as astronomer Sir Fred Hoyle predicted: "Once a photograph of the Earth, taken from the outside, is available..., a new idea as powerful as any in history will be let loose."[56]

This has been reinforced by TV flooding us daily with images of events in every part of the world. Suddenly, what is happening on the other side of the globe is as much in people's awareness as what is happening on the other side of town.

While cultural and national groupings still exist, they no longer form a relevant psychological boundary. In an incredibly short time span, man's traditional cultural and psychological borders have disappeared as a defining characteristic of his life.

And the painful issue facing us all is: "How am I going to adjust to this new condition? With whom do I identify? Who is my group? Indeed, do I have a group any longer?"

The answer, of course, is no; as a separate, isolated psychologically closed unit, all the groups we have known in the past have now been merged with one larger human family. As George Lucas, creator of the *Star Wars* trilogy, put it: "We began to perceive ourselves as a human race, as one world, one little ball of humanity. We had new information with which to go forward. Some people got scared, turned inward, became overwhelmed. Others saw."[57]

What each person is facing is the painful necessity to adjust to this new reality, and it will require, in the words of Christopher Fry, the British playwright, "the longest stride of soul men ever took."[58]

This new condition means identifying not just with what used to be one's group or nation, but with a larger humanity. It means an expansion of heart and spirit, so that each one of us grows to the point where we as individuals feel at home with people of every nation, race and culture.

Such expansion represents one of the greatest emotional and psychological stages of growth a person can experience. The difficulty, taking place in America as well as in many other parts of the world, of breaking through to this new consciousness is exemplified by resurging attempts to identify with one's former group.

In light of this need for such a giant step forward in human awareness, and in light of the increasing fragmentation of America into multiplying ethnic, sexual, regional and parochial groups, what does the future hold for America?

That is a legitimate question, but almost impossible to answer. Scenarios could be developed where America becomes so chocked by multiculturalism that consensus on how to deal with common problems becomes impossible. In such a case, America could stagnate and lose any sense of common purpose and identity.

Or America might just limp along with the minimum amount of consensus needed to keep vital functions in operation. The country doesn't break down, but neither does it rise to the new challenges facing it and the world. Such a state would have profound implications for the rest of the world, as well as for America.

The prevailing sense of insecurity and pessimism in America, particularly among the *intelligentsia*, would predict one of these two outcomes.

There is a deep reservoir of heart and spirit in the American people, however, that holds the promise of another possibility for the future. The America of Jefferson and Lincoln, even the America of Stevenson and Eisenhower, may be gone, but that does not mean that the spirit that animated such men does not yet still live deep within the soul of the American people.

Jefferson and Lincoln gave expression to fundamental human truths. They were not American truths, nor were they European truths. Liberty is not an American idea, and the free-market economy is not solely an American invention. Neither did human dignity enter the world with the Declaration of Independence. Certain qualities of life belong not to any one group of people, but to the human family as a whole. Such modes of life may have been more pronounced in one part of the world than another at some particular time, but this is part of the unfolding design of history, not the result of some supposed genius of a particular people. Various gifts of Providence may have been given through one specific people or another, but such gifts are given for the benefit of all humankind.

So in this sense, it is possible to see an America emerge that takes liberty, self-government, self-control and human dignity beyond the experience of the early Americans or the probing geniuses of the Enlightenment. Such new visions of cooperative living may come from the descendents of the original European settlers of the American continent.

But it is equally possible that such new life could be sparked by the Afro-Americans who have known a different part of the American experience. Or it may be the people of Spanish descent, who in bringing to America the richness of several traditions and cultures, ignite new fires deep within the American soul.

Or the new Americans from Vietnam, Korea, Taiwan or other parts of Asia could be the agents that infuse new meaning into the American Experiment at a new point in its trajectory. The spirit that animates the Native-Americans is already seeping into the country's consciousness to a degree not experienced in modern times, so the Native-Americans may yet speak to us all with a renewed dynamic of the Great Spirit.

But it's more likely that the new America would be a product not of any one group, but rather of individuals from all groups, having moved beyond the confines of their group identity, cooperating in a manner not yet seen on the North American continent.

If this third possibility were to materialize, then a true Universal Nation would indeed emerge. And that new Universal Nation would have something to offer a shrinking, multicultural world — something as relevant for this age as were the offerings of Jefferson and his contemporaries for their times just over two centuries ago.

CHAPTER EIGHT

THE AMERICAN FUTURE

There is today among many thoughtful observers a belief that the modern age is drawing to a close, that the sequence of events that began around the year 1500 has nearly run its course... Civilized human society has reached a point where it must change its habits if it is to survive.

Lynton Caldwell

At the beginning of this book, we spoke of a nation in upheaval in every department of its life. Such massive change has many effects. It brings in new and better ways of conducting day-to-day affairs, it opens new horizons of possibility, and it eases some of life's burdens so that people are able to enjoy a fuller existence.

But change also creates insecurity. Change is a departure from known ways, and it confronts one with an horizon of the unknown. Most people have protective instincts, so the desire for security prompts them to stick with habits and traditions rather than venture down an unknown path.

Insecurity creates fear, and this combined insecurity and fear greatly influence the attitudes and activities of America today. The whole world order is changing. So what is America's future world role? That is a major unknown, and it is unsettling. The globalization of world financial markets and the speed at which they operate have introduced an element of insecurity into our financial system; and that financial system itself is not secure.

America is confronted with industrial competition never faced before, primarily from Japan, but from other nations as well. Coupled with the restructuring of American industry that has taken place this past decade, as well as with the increased technology in the manufacturing process, this new competition has brought insecurity into the job market. Job security is often far more important in labor negotiations than wage increases.

The home and school increasingly fail to instill the qualities of character and citizenship that provide responsibility and coherence as a collective enterprise, so people fear for America's very future as a nation. The church and synagogue seem less able to provide the eternal certainties that used to give people an anchor in life and a clear sense of their place in the larger universal order. Communications and technology have accelerated life's tempo and, to many, events seem out of control.

The very structure of the family, the foundation of all social life, is being altered, to so great a degree that children are denied the love and family stability that create inner security.

To understand America today, we have to assess this underlying insecurity that pervades every area of life. It may appear more dramatic in an inner city neighborhood where a parent fears for her child's physical safety, but it's just as apparent in the boardrooms of some of America's giant global corporations. Corporate executives may project a "tough" image; but when a Salomon Brothers betrays its premier position, when an IBM restructures in such a basic manner, when giant banks disappear overnight, uncertainty and insecurity are present despite corporate achievement.

And people who are insecure or fearful will frequently act in ways unconsciously designed to compensate for that insecurity. This is the source of much of the aggressiveness, insensitivity and, yes, Japan-bashing, that allies in Japan and Europe witness in America today.

Uncertainty and insecurity, however, are not new to Americans. The people who risked their lives in the dangerous ocean trips to come to America in the 18th and 19th centuries certainly knew fear and insecurity. The Americans who left the Eastern seaboard and walked across the mountains and the Western wilderness to create a new life for themselves clearly were walking into an unknown future. The men and women who settled America were people of courage and character who, despite the insecurities involved, reached out for that unknown future, grasped it in their hands, and forged the mightiest industrial and military nation the world has known.

What was the common factor with all these early Americans? That, wherever they came from and whatever their station in life, they intended to build something new. Some had grand visions of empire building. Others had smaller aspirations of simply finding some rich farmland and developing it. But all had a sense of reaching forward into the unknown and creating something new out of the opportunities at hand.

And that is exactly where America stands today — at the edge of the unknown, on the threshold of limitless opportunity. Once again Americans are challenged to reach forward into that unknown, to grasp opportunity in their hands and to build something new for themselves, for their children, and, perhaps, for the world.

This challenge is of far greater difficulty than the task faced by George Washington and Thomas Jefferson. Their job was to make a nation out of the nearly four million people, who were of common northern European heritage, in a static agricultural setting where people and information could move no faster than the speed of a horse.

The task today is to give new meaning and direction to a nation of 250 million people (roughly the population of the entire world at the time of Julius Caesar), of multicultural origin, living in a dynamic urban setting, where nationhood is defined in a global context, with information moving instantaneously from one part of the world to another.

It is a commonly understood phenomenon, among historians and sociologists, that civilizations frequently falter because they emphasize certain human characteristics originally essential to their success. A point is reached in a nation's evolution, partially as a result of external circumstances, when different human qualities must come into play to take a people to their next stage of development.

Such a juncture requires a reassessment of underlying assumptions. Without such a reassessment, a nation continues to look at events within a context no longer relevant, and it thus deals with symptoms rather than with basic realities.

America stands at just such a juncture. Its future depends not on technological fixes or on over-intellectualized policy analysis, but on the readiness of Americans to rethink underlying assumptions about personal life, social organization, and collective purpose, and to adjust where necessary.

Assumption Number One: That because totalitarianism appears to have collapsed in the former Soviet Union (it has at least imploded in its Communist imperial form), freedom is automatically the wave of the future in Russia, Eastern Europe and the world.

Such an assumption is based on a limited assessment of the requirements for maintaining freedom.

A more realistic assumption is that freedom is not simply a political system that can be grafted mechanically on to any body politic; freedom is one of the most advanced states of the human spirit. Freedom is far more than the absence of political or physical restraint. A nation might possess the political structures of freedom, while at the same time lose the moral and psychological subsoil in which freedom grows. For this reason, every generation must create the self-restraint and the inner spiritual essence that give freedom its vitality and dynamism, if freedom is to prosper under changing conditions.

Certainly the masses of people in Moscow and St. Petersburg who defied the August 1991 *putsch* reversed a thousand years of Russian history in that they showed that the Russian people would no longer submit to an authoritarian rule, be it a Czar or a Commissar.

But denying domination is only the beginning of freedom. The more difficult phase is creating the public motivations and attitudes which inspire a people to rise above personal and parochial interests, and be responsible for a larger common good.

At its core, freedom is a political manifestation of a psychological or spiritual condition. It is rooted in the depths of the individual personality. The wellspring of liberty is the creative and elevating expression of purpose that flows from each person maintaining unbroken contact with their inner-most selves. Freedom is the product of a people's capacity to go to the core of their souls, and to evoke constantly new and ennobling patterns of meaning and significance.

A person is only free when they feel that, at the very core of their being, is an affirmation of life that is indestructible by any external power — be it force, affluence or public opinion.[59]

Whenever such psychological conditions do not prevail, the exercise of freedom — both politically and personally — becomes dysfunctional. It is in this context that the difficulty of America's federal government, both Congress and the Executive Branch, to conduct the nation's business must be viewed. Over the past three decades, parochial interests have increasingly frustrated effective execution of the national interest. Thus, for at least 25 years, political leaders have talked about America's deteriorating infrastructure, the growing "underclass," the low savings rate, the decreasing educational performance, the lack of control of the federal budget, and much more. But all the talk has produced disappointing results.

The dysfunction of American freedom can also be seen in problems arising in the body politic at-large. Americans are not free of stress and anxiety (the fastest growing component of institutional health care programs). We are not free of boredom (a major cause of drugs and violence). We are not free of addiction in its many forms. We are not free of cynicism and despair, which are principal themes of America's culture. We are not free of fear — fear of failure, of what people think, of losing control. We are not free of the loneliness which, psychologists say, has reached epidemic proportions.

While such problems have always plagued every society to a certain extent, they now threaten the individual psychological substructure which is the very foundation of American freedom. What is at stake is not simply individual happiness; it is the psychological ability of a people to exercise freedom responsibly.

What is needed is not simply freedom from governmental regulation and inhibiting social attitudes. More than that, America needs a new cultural climate and a collective sense of mission that encourage us to renew contact with the deepest parts of our inner selves. From this can come a sense of destiny that will allow us to reach beyond ourselves, to strive for some larger common good.

Americans need once again to be ready to stake our "lives, fortunes and sacred honor" to take America's experiment with freedom to its next stage. Someone needs to decide that, whatever the personal cost, he or she will do for America now what Madison, Jefferson and others did for an earlier period.

So America is at a point where a fundamental rethinking of the assumptions about freedom is needed — what it is, what makes it work, what ensures its continuance. (Note that this not only pertains to America. These questions are at the core of the struggle of Eastern Europe and the

Commonwealth of Independent States to establish democracy and a free economic system.)

Assumption Number Two: That the underlying attitudes and perspectives that have created economic wealth thus far are adequate for the future.

They are not. No existing economic theory explains the events of the past two decades. Reality is outrunning theory.

Every earlier theory stipulated that one economic universe controls all economic activity. Earlier economic theories also ignored resource-depletion, health-related concerns, the needs of mothers in the workplace, externalities such as educating the workforce or "white-collar" crime, and environmental damage. Hiring 10,000 people to clean up the Alaskan oil spill shows up as a plus for Alaska's economy. Nor have technology's development, the "invisible" economy, innovation or entrepreneurship been factored into our economic models. At an even deeper level, economic models ignore factors such as cultural values and differences, social costs and human development and fulfillment.

The new assumption must be based on the reality that there are several economic spheres — a "microeconomy" of individuals and corporations; a "macroeconomy" of national governments; a "world economy" that includes the interactions of nations, global corporations and financial institutions; and now regional economies of the European Community, the North American Free Trade Zone and the Pacific Basin, which seem to be developing as well.

Any new assumption must include all these elements. It must go beyond short-term variables, and look at the long-term total environment — at creating and maintaining the right conditions for living as well as a strong and healthy economy. Economic assumptions must now become qualitative as well as quantitative. The starting place is the awareness that the economy rests on ecology, and that this planet must be left in at least as good, if not better, condition for future generations.

Even more fundamentally, the new assumption must understand that economic prosperity does not create a great civilization. Rather, the discipline of building a great civilization — with all its potential and restraints — is what generates wealth and economic growth.

As France's Albert Bressand wrote about the world economy in *Foreign Affairs* some time ago: "Our present crisis is one of values, worldviews and economic philosophy — before being one of policies and indicators. Getting back on the prosperity track requires not only a 'conceptual breakthrough' at the policy level but also a capacity we seem to have lost for rediscovering the fundamental values we have in common."[60]

The new economic assumptions will grow out of those values which the world community must hold in common if it's to function as a community.

Such values must include, but not necessarily be limited to:

> Long-term viability of the ecosystem.
> Work as an expression of human fulfillment and dignity.
> Personal integrity as the principal operating requirement of <u>any</u> production or financial system.
> Individual initiative.
> Mutual interdependence.
> Material sufficiency.

"Conceptual breakthroughs" at the policy level must be based on what might be considered such a new global economic ethic.

<u>Assumption Number Three</u>: That with a few changes such as increasing teachers' salaries, adding longer school hours, increasing math and science studies, enhancing parental choice and giving students more homework, America's educational system will truly prepare America's young people for the 21st century.

As necessary as some of these changes may be, such an assumption is questionable, at best.

The American educational system was designed for an era that no longer exists. It was designed for an agricultural/industrial era where population shifts were relatively slow; where educational institutions were the primary source of information for children; where ethnic diversity was minimal; where children's political awareness was, at best, national in scope; where there was a strong sense of national identity; where the family was the primary source of value inculcation and character forma- tion; and where Americans shared some common spiritual orientation. Again, these circumstances are gone.

The new assumption is that education must be redefined for a period of history unlike anything the human race has ever experienced. In an age when children get more information from watching TV than they do from sixteen years of classroom instruction, when all knowledge is available by the press of a computer button, when commercial advertising has become the primary source of value formation, the basic questions need to be asked, "What is education? What is a minimal educational experience for this age? What is the product education seeks to produce?"

Given the rational/logical base of an "Information Society," and given the increasing use of computers in schools, if education is to produce balanced personalities, it must start with the premise that its initial task is to awaken the child to the wonder and mystery of life, and to develop the child's intuitive as well as rational capacities.

Indeed, we could make Thomas Carlyle's observation the foundation of education for an Information Age: "One grand, invaluable secret there is which includes all the rest," he noted, "and lies clearly in every man's power: To have an open, loving heart, and what follows from the possession of such."

Continued Carlyle: "Truly, it has been said: A loving Heart is the beginning of all Knowledge. This it is that opens the whole mind, quickens every faculty of the intellect to do its fit work — that of knowing — and therefore, by sure consequence, of vividly uttering-forth."[61]

Obviously, American children must be educated in the traditional academic subjects so that they are at least equal to the best in the world. But if America is moving into a new period of its development, education must equip American children to grapple with life's fundamental questions. Questions such as the following:

What is at the core of liberty, and how is it sustained? In a society where the primary value source (TV) is collective, how does a child develop his or her individual sense of being, yet relate that being to some larger responsibility for the community? In an age of mobility and global TV impressions, what can be found to help us realize a sense of roots and our unique position in both time and place? What does a student need to know when there is so much that can be known? How does one gain self-understanding, self-control and self-direction? What gives life its highest signifi-cance, and what saves it from meaninglessness?

If these questions seem remote or abstract to you, consider one student speaker at a recent Stanford University graduation. He described his class as "not knowing how it relates to the past or the future, having little sense of the present, no life-sustaining beliefs, secular or religious," and, consequently, "no goal and no path of effective action."[62]

Such questions are not easily answered. But a people who cannot answer them cannot sustain a civilized life of liberty. Yet teaching young people to create the conditions of a civilized life of liberty ought to be the primary aim of education.

Assumption Number Four: That reality, especially scientific reality, amounts to what can be measured, reduced to its constituent parts, verified by repeated experiment, and observed in objective detachment; and that mind or consciousness are a result of physical or chemical processes taking place in the brain. Such assumptions have been the basis of the Newtonian worldview, a worldview of certainty and predictability.

The new assumption is that we are well into a Quantum Age of uncertainty and unpredictability; that in the realm of quantum mechanics, an "objective experiment" is a contradiction in terms; that the physical world may not consist of structures built out of independently existing (and unanalyzable) entities, but rather a web of relationships between elements whose meanings arise wholly from their link to the whole; that a complete understanding of reality lies outside the capabilities of rational thought, and must include subjective, intuitive insights; that conscious-ness/mind did not appear late in the evolutionary process, but were always here; that far from mind being housed in the brain, mind exists independently of the brain, and possibly independently of the body; and that subatomic particles may contain some form of consciousness which enables them to transmit knowledge faster than the speed of light, over distances measured by light-years.

The above assumptions form the greatest shift of scientific worldview since Galileo's work in the 17th century. Despite their startling implications, they evolved throughout the past century — and yet still have to work their way through the philosophy, knowledge structure, culture, education and general worldview of the rest of American society. But the process of these new assumptions asserting their authority is at the very base of today's upheaval.[63]

<u>Assumption Number Five</u>: That if America's young people are filled with a vacuous and violent culture through TV, rock music lyrics, cinema and literature, they can function properly when they take their place in society.

The new assumption is that for America to prepare itself for a new stage of its experience, a new culture must be created that inspires Americans to great endeavor. America's "culture-shapers" must begin to express themes that will compel an entire generation to reach forward for a new age. New motifs must be expressed in music, TV, cinema and literature — motifs that display the promise and possibility of the future, not simply the failures of the past or the hypocrisies of the present.

In sum, our culture must draw forth what is highest in the American character, and relate these qualities to the building of a new period of history. Such a new cultural atmosphere is the *sine qua non* for any worthwhile move toward an educational environment geared to the 21st-century needs.

Perhaps the need for this new culture was best expressed by Pope John Paul II when he met with 1,500 representatives of the movie, television, recording and newspaper industries: "All the media of popular culture which you represent can build or destroy, uplift or cast down. You have untold possibilities for good, ominous possibilities for destruction. It is the difference between death and life — the death or life of the spirit. And it is a matter of choice. The challenge of Moses to the people of Israel is applicable to all of us today: 'I set before you life and death... Choose life.'"[64]

<u>Assumption Number Six</u>: That leadership is about the exercise of power (defined as the ability to get others to conform to the leader's will); that leadership is making the "tough decisions," being "in control" and bringing people and events into alignment with a predetermined outcome.

This is one concept of leadership, and it dominates American politics and corporate affairs. But, despite our best efforts, such leadership is not producing the results the times require.

The new assumption is that an America moving into a new phase of its experience requires a new form of leadership. This new leadership is driven by the fact that the information/wisdom gap between leaders and led has been virtually eliminated — thanks to instant and universal information. The new leadership is, in fact, based on a change in the very nature of power.

The core of the new leadership is vision. Vision is seeing beyond the immediacy of the day. It is understanding the temper of the times, the outlines of the future, and how to move from one to the other. Vision is seeing where life is headed, and how to make the transition from here to there most effectively. Vision is seeing what life could be like while dealing with life as it is. Vision is having some sense of the inner impulse of the Age. It is sensing what is felt, yet unarticulated, in the public soul — and then giving it voice. Vision is seeing the potential purpose hidden in the chaos of the moment, yet which could bring to birth new possibilities for a people. Vision deals with those deeper human intangibles which alone give ultimate purpose to life. In the end, vision must always deal with life's qualities, not its quantities.

The mission of leadership is to align people with some vision in such a manner as to permit the full range of their capacities to contribute to the realization of that vision. The new leadership must use all the conventional leadership qualities of energy, decisiveness, technical competence, intelligence and specialized experience.

But the new leadership must go beyond those qualities and draw on sides of the human character not normally associated with leadership — empathy, openness, flexibility, sensitivity to Life's natural rhythm, and, above all, intuition. For intuition is the primary source of wisdom — each person's link with "nonrational reality" which, as quantum mechanics is teaching us, affects events every bit as much as does perceived reality.

The new leadership's essence is getting one's ego out of the way so that the unused potential of the intuitive faculties are free to inform the rational mind and permit solutions to emerge. America faces no problem for which there isn't a solution. Solutions are inherent in the order of Life, for solutions are that condition where the state of events is in natural balance. Finding solutions is usually frustrated by the intercession of ego or personal attitudes and agendas.

Thus leadership is creating the climate where personal ego and attitudes are minimized, and where the natural order is free to find its equilibrium. Among other things, Leadership is about "letting go" and allowing the natural rhythm of Life to predominate.

Rethinking assumptions about leadership may be the determining factor in how quickly and effectively America surmounts the trials of transition, and builds the relationships and structures on which her future depends.

<u>Assumption Number Seven</u>: That the "pursuit of happiness" automatically means increasing the accumulation of cars, computers, VCRs and compact discs; that an increase in the "gross national product" equates with an advance in "gross national happiness."

How could an entire nation have been beguiled into believing this? Despite Americans possessing greater material wealth today than any people ever possessed in the long story of mankind, psychologists say alienation, depression and an absence of meaning characterize far too many American lives. Such a condition is reflected in our national culture — which wouldn't project such psychotic themes if they didn't resonate with what's going on in people's inner lives.

So what's the new assumption? It is that despite the fact that the right to happiness is written into the Declaration of Independence, happiness itself cannot be conferred on a people by a state document, nor can it be achieved through the accumulation of material goods. Happiness seems to be unattainable as a primary aim in life. Rather, it is more the by-product of the quality of one's living and the purpose for which one lives.

Happiness appears to require a goal outside of, and larger than one's self if it is to be achieved. The key to happiness appears to be the quality of one's being, not the quantity of one's having. In light of this, Americans must now discover some larger purpose than personal accumulation of wealth and expansion of the gross national product.

Assumption Number Eight: That America's problems are basically the result of impersonal economic, technological and social forces external to the individual; that the individual is a victim of events rather than a participant shaping events.

This is a half-truth, if that much. The more accurate assumption is that the problems of an Age are never simply "out there" somewhere; they always, in part, reflect what is taking place inside the heart and soul of a nation's people. If the Age is disordered, this signals disorder in the human spirit.

Such disorder is not necessarily born of malign intent, but it is more likely caused by the disintegration of one way of viewing life and reality, while a new perspective of viewing existence has not yet taken shape.

America is in the midst of perhaps the greatest opening up of vistas and possibilities in history. It is one of the most difficult, exhilarating and wondrous times in which anyone could hope to live.

Yet life is changing so rapidly that old certainties are breaking down; people are adrift on a sea of meta- physical confusion. In a sense, the tectonic plates of life are shifting, and old moorings are no longer holding people securely.

In such a gyrating world, there is need for a sense of meaning that enables each of us to know who we are, why we're here, what we're rooted in, and what we're living for. Such knowledge is at the very core of any human community — be it a family, a corporation or a nation.

The issues facing America are, partially, the result of a disconnect, a disconnect with the deepest roots of the individual's inner being. That disconnect involves the rational and nonrational parts of the human personality. The rational side of our personality has been so cultivated that we can absorb massive amounts of data, and can manage the most complex mechanical and bureaucratic systems. America's whole technological structure is built on such rationality and logic.

But the nonrational side has been neglected, and this is the side that has historically developed art, culture and life's spiritual meanings. This is also the side that links people to the deeper rhythm of the natural world. Because this side has not been developed, America seems to be unable to provide a depth to life that links the individual to some larger significance beyond material gain, technical achievement or personal advancement. One result: The quality of American freedom is diminished, even as it is extended.

Given this neglect of the nonrational side of life, the basic issue now facing us is how to foster belief; belief in ourselves, in each other, in our future, in a common ethos, in what the founders of America called "Divine Providence," in a new and greater expression of life and human personality. For it is belief, and the habits and attitudes that belief engenders, that lifts a nation to a higher level of awareness and achievement. Without common belief, there is no civilized life. Such belief is the prerequisite for successfully moving into a new phase of the American experience; belief plus hope — for hope is the vision of possibility.

That is what the American people want — the vision of a new stage of the American Experiment. Such a vision cannot consist of an exhortation aimed at solving America's many difficult prob- lems, for that will not lift the American spirit to high endeavor.

A new vision must be based on the building of a new time, the creation of something America has never known before, both at home and in the world. The Age calls for an overwhelming undertaking that sets American hearts on fire.

We have entered a dimension of human and technical possibility that we have not yet begun to assimilate into our thinking and dreaming. We stand at the opening of one of the grand vistas of human achievement, as well as of human possibility. The call is to create a new civilization out of the new material and circumstances at hand.

<u>Assumption Number Nine</u>: That America is the world's only superpower and, as such, can unilaterally provide the leadership a new global order of affairs requires.

That would be a questionable reading of events. True, America is the only nation capable of projecting significant military force to almost any point on the globe. The U.S. Navy has virtually total command of the world's oceans, the first time in modern history any nation has such naval domination on such a scale. The stabilizing influence of American power is certainly felt in northeastern Asia, in the Middle East and, to a lesser extent, in Europe.

But true superpower status which, in any event, is a relative concept, includes a predominant global economic and political dimension as well as a military component. In 1946, America possessed the economic power to shape the post-war international order. In 1956, America's political muscle was strong enough to force Great Britain and France out of Suez. But in 1991, America could not have achieved the objectives of Desert Storm without the technological genius of Japan, as well as the financial help of Japan, Germany and many other nations.

The rise of other centers of economic and political power has changed the character of America's relationship to the rest of the world, as well as the nature of the leadership America must exercise. So underlying assumptions must be rethought.

The new assumption is that American leadership is pivotal to the emergence of whatever form of world community is evolving; that America is the major world power, but no longer a hegemon; and that future progress will require more than the unilateral leadership that, essentially, America effectively employed during the Cold War period.

The announcement by the United States of a *New World Order* illustrates the point. With the collapse of the former Soviet Union as an apparent security threat to the world, with the Commonwealth of Independent States unlikely to manipulate client states in proxy confrontations with the U.S. or its allies, and with the rise of nuclear Third World nations, there is indeed a new state of affairs in the world. So how will security and order be maintained?

That vital issue affects all nations. The answer, however, is not for the United States unilaterally to declare a *New World Order,* which has general implications but lacks conceptual contributions from other nations who will have to help implement it.

Some conceptual framework is obviously needed to define the new world order that has been emerging for several decades. But such a grand concept should be developed cooperatively at least by Japan, Germany, Great Britain, France, China and Russia, as well as the United States. If nations are expected to participate in maintaining a stable and secure structure for the new world order, they should have a part in defining what that new order consists of, and how it will be enforced.

More fundamentally, the issue is more than conventional security. The issue is the emergence of a new stage of world development. Security cannot be considered by itself. All issues are now intertwined. As Henry Kissinger noted, there is "a range of subjects that has never previously been the topic of global arrangements... It is the new agenda of population, environment and nuclear proliferation... [T]hese problems are so unprecedented, so complex and so global in their implications that international order begins to merge into a challenge to domestic governance."[65]

The highest order of leadership is needed for the period into which the world has now moved. But in light of the diffusion of both military and economic powers, the *New World Order* must be the creation of the best efforts of several nations taking a new degree of joint responsibility. For America, as Zbigniew Brzezinski noted, "More emphasis will have to be placed on cooperation with genuine partners, including shared decision-making in world security issues."[66] Lack of such a shift in America's mentality and operations will only encourage the "stick-it-in-your-eye" attitude shown by Germany towards the U.S. over recog- nition of Slovenia and Croatia.[67]

This is a unique time for America and Japan to combine their imagination and efforts — especially in light of Japan's beginning to define, in a new way, its global responsibilities. Despite each country's internal difficulties, despite our trade and cultural differences, Japan and America are the two nations with the most effective industrial and financial global outreach. They are therefore the two countries best suited to provide a sense of stability during a decade increasingly characterized by instability.

Perhaps one aspect of America's new world role is to act as a catalyst that encourages several nations to consider how, together, a new order of affairs is established for a new period of world development. America must provide the core strength in maintaining security where common world interests are involved.

Beyond that, America's traditional idealism can ignite a worldwide spirit of purposeful, creative adventure. For any new order of affairs, especially at the start of a new phase of the world's experience, will have to be based on more than the sum of national economic interests. To deal with multiple crises, as well as make use of incomprehensible opportunities, a fresh burst of vitality and life will have to infuse the conduct of affairs.

That historic American sense of reaching forward for new horizons can be one of America's most significant contributions to shaping this new Age.

Such contributions require the finest that is in the American people. In the words of Walt Whitman:

> *Now understand me well — it is provided in the essence of things that from any fruition of success, no matter what, shall come forth something to make a greater struggle necessary.*[68]

We Americans have experienced unparalleled political, material and technological success in our short lifetime. We must now call forth our deepest inner resources to grapple with this "greater struggle."

And that is the context for understanding the challenges confronting you and me today.

EPILOGUE

There is a meaning trying to achieve itself through history... a thrust underneath which is trying to make life more complete, to take this immense diversity of life and make it integrated, and make it into a greater and more creative whole.

Laurens van der Post

In these pages, we've covered much territory together. We've considered the American condition from many aspects. Yet much was left unsaid.

One parting thought: It's never been given to Americans to confront more than we can ultimately achieve. What we must do for our country now is not beyond our capacity. It's mainly a question of will, of decision and direction, and of acting together.

Taking America into its next stage of fulfillment is not going to happen in one great moment. No magic formula is on hand to transform our condition.

What would George Washington and Thomas Jefferson do if they were here now? No one really knows. But they would probably look to the fundamentals of human behavior and social conduct. They would possibly delineate the broader themes which enable a people to cohere. Most likely, they would take the longer and wider view of our prospects.

And they would in some way provide a heart, a soul, a conscience, to our efforts. For they knew that the American experiment combines practicality of action with nobility of spirit.

Yet, however much we may wish it, no George or Tom has shown up to help. What confronts us now must be done, or at least started, by you and by me. It's that simple. Each of us can take certain steps. They range from simple decisions about the standards with which we govern our personal lives, to carrying out professional responsibilities in an enhanced manner, to perhaps participating in the public arena in a way we never considered.

Whatever it is, if we stop and listen to that inner voice that prompts the human heart forward, all of us sense certain steps — immediate and practical — that would make a difference. While it may not seem like a nation-shaping action, the cumulative effect of all of us taking his or her special step will begin building a new America.

And the building of that new America may depend, in part, on the emphasis given this basic question:

What is the ultimate meaning of America? Is it the performance of our technology, or the quality of our people?

As said at the outset, you and I live in a time of unprecedented trial. Such times can call forth the highest and finest in us. Such times require that we go beyond the conventional, that we break through the sound barrier to a fresh stage of existence. Few generations are permitted to live through such times. It's dangerous, but exciting; uncertain, but full of hidden possibility; painful, but then so is the birth of new life.

And that's what we have the chance to achieve — to live and to act together on such a plane that new life is infused into every aspect of the American Experiment.

Thank you for travelling these pages with me. And remember: If you'd like to write me about thoughts that resulted from you're reading of this book, your letter (or FAX note) will be most welcome.

NOTES

1 J. Hector St. John de Crevecoeur, *Letters From an American Farmer*, Penguin Books 1981.

2 Francis Bradley, *The American Proposition*, Princeton University Press 1977, p. 79.

3 Ibid., p. 55.

4 James Truslow Adams, *The Epic of America*, Little, Brown and Co. 1931.

5 Ibid.

6 Ibid.

7 Ibid.

8 *Long-Term Economic Growth*, U.S. Department of Commerce 1973.

9 John Lukacs, *Outgrowing Democracy: A History of the United States in the 20th Century*, Doubleday & Company Inc. 1984.

10 Frederick Turner, *Rediscovering America*, Viking 1985.

11 Ibid.

12 John Lukacs, *Outgrowing Democracy: A History of the United States in the Twentieth Century*, Doubleday % Company Inc. 1984.

13 Frederick Turner, *Rediscovering America*, Viking 1985.

14 *Inaugural Addresses of the Presidents of the United States*, U.S. Government Printing Office 1989, p. 228.

15 Walter Lippmann, *A Preface to Morals*, Time-Life Books 1964, p. 104.

16 Robert Nisbet, *The Present Age*, Harper and Row 1988.

17 Frederick Turner, *Rediscovering America*, Viking 1985.

18 Theodore H. White, *In Search of History*, Harper and Row 1978.

19 Adlai Stevenson, Commencement Address at Columbia University: June 5, 1954.

20 Rollo May, *Love and Will*, Dell Publishing Co. 1969, p.27.

21 Lewis Mumford, *Interpretations and Forecasts 1922-1972*, Harvest/HGB 1979, p. 480.

22 Theodore White, *In Search of History*, Harper and Row 1978.

23 Ibid.

24 William Shakespeare, *Macbeth*.

25 Alexander Hellemans and Bryan Bunch, *Time Tables of Science*, Simon and Schuster 1988, p. 490.

26 Joseph S. Nye, Jr., *Bound to Lead*, Basic Books Inc. 1990, p. 15.

27 Ben Wattenberg, *The First Universal Nation*, The Free Press 1991, p. 370.

28 Employment and Earnings, *Bureau of Labor Statistics*, U.S. Department of Labor, July 1991.

29 Tvina Mohorovic, Dun and Bradstreet.

30 George Gilder, "Freedom and the High-Tech Revolution," *Imprimis*, November 1990, Vol. 19, No. 11.

31 Ibid.

32 Ibid.

33 Ben Wattenberg, *The First Universal Nation*, The Free Press 1991, p. 121.

34 Ibid.

35 Ibid, p. 116.

36 Ibid, p. 116.

37 James Patterson and Peter Kim, *The Day America Told the Truth*, Prentice Hall Press 1991, p. 231.

38 C.G. Jung, *Civilization in Transition*, Princeton University Press 1970, p. 228.

39 Neil Postman, "The Antidote to Trivialization," *New Perspectives Quarterly*, Fall 1990, Vol. 7, No. 4. Also see *Amusing Ourselves to Death* by Neil Postman, Penguin Books 1985.

40 See Joshua Meyrowitz, "Television: The Shared Arena," *The World & I*, July 1990.

41 Robert Goldberg, "Television," *The Wall Street Journal*, January 2, 1990.

42 See Joshua Meyrowitz, "Television: The Shared Arena," *The World & I*, July 1990.

43 George Gilder, "Freedom and the High-Tech Revolution," *Imprimis*, November 1990, Vol. 19, No. 11.

44 See Sherry Turkle, *The Second Self*, Simon and Schuster Inc. 1985. Also see Joshua Meyrowitz, *No Sense of Place*, Oxford University Press 1985.

45 Ibid.

46 Comment made in a personal conversation with the author at the Lindbergh Fund Annual Award Dinner, Paris 1987.

47 Ben Wattenberg, *The First Universal Nation*, The Free Press 1991, p. 121.

48 Joel Kotkin, "The Demographic Limits of 'Great Powers'," *CEO International Strategies*, July/August 1991.

49 Paul Gray, "Whose America?,"*Time*, July 8, 1991.

50 Ibid.

51 Ibid.

52 Ibid.

53 Ibid.

54 Craig Lambert, "Global Spin," *Harvard Magazine*, January/February 1990.

55 Paul Gray, "Whose America?," *Time,* July 8, 1991.

56 Sir Fred Hoyle, quoted in *The Global Brain*, P. Hussell, Los Angeles: J.P. Tarcher 1983.

57 George Lucas, Interview in *Rolling Stone*, November/ December 1987.

58 *Christopher Fry Plays*, Oxford University Press 1971.

59 The author is indebted to Mihajlo Mihajlov for some of these insights.

60 Albert Bressand, "Mastering The World Economy," *Foreign Affairs*, Spring 1983.

61 Thomas Carlyle, "Biography," in *Critical and Miscellaneous Essays Vol III*, Chapman and Hall Ltd. 1899.

62 Rollo May, *The Cry For Myth*, W.W. Norton & Company Inc. 1991.

63 See *The Emperor's New Mind* by Roger Penrose, Penguin Books 1989. Also see *Creative Work* by Willis Harman and John Hormon, Knowledge Systems Inc. 1989.

64 *The New York Times*, September 16, 1987.

65 Henry Kissinger, *The Washington Post,* December 3, 1991.

66 Zbigniew Brzezinski, "Selective Global Commitment," *Foreign Affairs*, Vol. 70, No. 4, 1991.

67 See "Germany's Europe," by Rowland Evans and Robert Novak, *The Washington Post*, December 20, 1991.

68 Walt Whitman, *Leaves of Grass*, The New American Library 1955, p. 144.

ABOUT THE AUTHOR

Wm. Van Dusen Wishard heads **WorldTrends Research,** a consultancy offering corporations, professional associations and educators an integrated frame of reference for decision-making.

For two decades, Van Wishard has written and lectured on the broad trends reshaping the global landscape. His address to Members of Congress attending a **Congressional Institute** conference was televised nationally. A Japanese edition of his book, *A Perspective For The '90s,* made the best-seller list of business books sold in Japan. Mr. Wishard's assessment of how corporations respond to the changing social and political environment was published by the **McGraw-Hill Publishing Company** as part of the book *Corporations At The Crossroads.* His published analysis of the 1970s was described by *The Washington Post* as "the most incisive com- mentary on the 1970s yet seen."

The Prime Minister of Japan directed that Van Wishard's survey of world trends, *Perspective '87,* be used in a staff study of world trends affecting Japan. Wishard's analyses have appeared in journals from the *Christian Science Monitor* to *The Futurist* to *The Japan Times.*

Van Wishard entered U.S. government service in 1970, eventually serving in four administrations. Throughout the 1980s he was the Special Assistant to the Secretary and the Deputy Secretary of the **U.S. Department of Commerce.** In this capacity he wrote on U.S. competitiveness, international trade and economic policy. Prior to 1970, he worked in over 30 countries with non-profit public-information and education programs, and in 1965 helped found **Up With People.**

He is an Associate Fellow of New York's **Omega Group,** an Adjunct Fellow of the Congressional Institute, and an Adjunct Fellow of the **Arlington Institute.** He is also a member of the **National Speakers Association.** Mr. Wishard served as an officer in the **U.S. Army** and received the Bronze Star while in Korea.

To Order <u>Additional Copies</u> of

The American Future (What Would George and Tom Do Now?)

Contact:

The Congressional Institute, Inc.
316 Pennsylvania Ave. S.E. #403
Washington, D.C. 20003-1167
(202) 547-4600 Fax (202) 547-3556

Single Copy	**$ 12.95**
2-10 copies	**11.95**
11-25	**10.95**
26-100	**9.95**
101 or more	***Please Call (202) 547-4600***

- -

Please send me ______ copies of:

The American Future (What Would George and Tom Do Now?)

I've enclosed $___.__ times _____ copies plus 10% for postage and handling for a total of $ ___.__. My copies will be shipped by ground transportation unless I add additional instructions and shipping fees.

NAME ______________________________

INSTITUTION ______________________________

ADDRESS ______________________________

CITY ____________________ **ST** _____ **ZIP** __________

Telephone: (_____) ______________________________

To Order <u>Additional Copies</u> of

The American Future (What Would George and Tom Do Now?)

Contact:

The Congressional Institute, Inc.
316 Pennsylvania Ave. S.E. #403
Washington, D.C. 20003-1167
(202) 547-4600 Fax (202) 547-3556

Single Copy	**$ 12.95**
2-10 copies	**11.95**
11-25	**10.95**
26-100	**9.95**
101 or more	***Please Call (202) 547-4600***

- -

Please send me ______ copies of:

The American Future

(What Would George and Tom Do Now?)

I've enclosed $___.__ times _____ copies plus 10% for postage and handling for a total of $ ___.__. My copies will be shipped by ground transportation unless I add additional instructions and shipping fees.

NAME ________________________________

INSTITUTION __________________________

ADDRESS _____________________________

CITY ________________ **ST** _____ **ZIP** _______

Telephone: (____) ________________________